D1635169

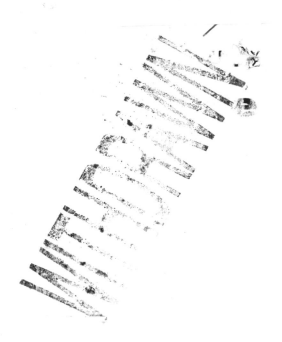

DIVERS · GREBES · SHEARWATERS · PETRELS ·
GANNET · CORMORANTS

HERONS · EGRET · BITTERNS · STORKS ·
SPOONBILL

DUCKS · GEESE · SWANS

BIRDS OF PREY: EAGLES · BUZZARDS · HAWKS ·
HARRIERS · OSPREY · FALCONS

GROUSE · PHEASANTS · PARTRIDGES · QUAIL ·
CRAKES · WATER RAIL · MOORHEN · COOT ·
CRANE · BUSTARDS

WADERS: OYSTERCATCHER · PLOVERS · SNIPE ·
CURLEWS · GODWITS · SANDPIPERS · SHANKS ·
AVOCET · STILT · PHALAROPES

SKUAS · GULLS · TERNS · AUKS

PIGEONS · OWLS · CUCKOO · NIGHTJAR ·
KINGFISHER · SWIFTS · BEE-EATER · ROLLER ·
HOOPOE · GOLDEN ORIOLE · WOODPECKERS

LARKS · SWALLOWS · CROWS · TITS · NUTHATCH ·
CREEPERS · WREN · DIPPER

THRUSHES · CHATS · STARTS · ROBIN ·
NIGHTINGALES

WARBLERS · CRESTS · DUNNOCK · FLYCATCHERS

PIPITS · WAGTAILS · SHRIKES · WAXWING ·
STARLINGS

FINCHES · BUNTINGS · SPARROWS

RARITIES

16-25

26-31

32-55

56-71

72-85

86-109

110-129

130-153

154-171

172-181

182-199

200-209

210-227

? 228-239

The Birdwatcher's Key

THE BIRDWATCHER'S KEY

*A guide to identification
in the field*

*382 species compiled
and described by*
Bob Scott
and illustrated by
Don Forrest

FREDERICK WARNE

Published by
FREDERICK WARNE (PUBLISHERS) LTD: LONDON
FREDERICK WARNE & CO INC: NEW YORK

First published 1976
Reprinted 1979
Reprinted 1980
Reprinted 1984

Cased Edition: ISBN 0 7232 1829 3
Limp Edition: ISBN 0 7232 1960 5

Text filmset by
BAS Printers Limited, Over Wallop, Hampshire
Colour reproductions & printing by
L. Van Leer & Co Ltd, Holland

D7221, 1283

Contents

How to use the Key

This book is primarily intended for use in the field as a quick handy aid to identification and has been specially designed to slip easily into the pocket. The birds illustrated are those that occur regularly in the region of north-west Europe covered by the Key (see p. 13), either as residents, summer or winter visitors, or annual passage migrants. Also included are a few of the more regular casual visitors or rarities.

With the bird to be identified before you, or the details you have noted fresh in your mind, turn to the inside front or back cover of the book. From the list of groups printed there, choose the one which most closely resembles the bird you wish to identify (e.g. duck, woodpecker, finch, etc.). Bend the pages as shown in the illustration below and opposite the group chosen you will find a coloured mark on the edge of the plates indicating where to find the illustrations of the birds in that group. The relevant text will be found facing the illustration.

If you are not sure to which group of birds your individual belongs, look among the small drawings provided for something of a similar shape and examine the plates it guides you to. If you still have not found your bird, examine all those groups of plates which are not obviously wrong. You will not find a long-legged wading bird among the finches and buntings, but a

thrush-sized bird running on the beach might turn out to be a Ringed Plover, to be found among the waders.

Do not overlook the possibility that your bird may be in immature plumage. Where there are marked differences between male and female, winter and summer, immature and adult plumages, these have been illustrated. Where no marked differences occur a single illustration is provided.

All the birds on one plate are drawn to the same scale and this is indicated by the single black line on the side of the plate which represents 15 cm (6″) to the scale of the plate. Note that the insets illustrating a particular feature or plumage and surrounded by a white line are drawn to a different scale to the main illustrations on that plate.

At each point in the text where a new family comprising several species commences, a short paragraph in italics describes the characteristics common to members of that family. The text does not include plumage characters obvious from the plates except in circumstances where a particular feature would assist with identification. As a further aid to quick identification, bold type in the text draws immediate attention to the more important diagnostic features. Where reference is made to a similar-looking species or a species with similar behaviour, the name of the bird is printed in small capitals the first time it is mentioned in the paragraph, followed by the page number if the species referred to appears on another page. Very familiar birds, such as robins and sparrows, are not cross-referenced for comparative purposes. The text also includes notes on distribution in north-west Europe, seasonal occurrences (also included in the Check List) and habitat, and these points should also be checked as an additional aid to identification.

The order of families and species followed in the Key is generally that of the *Wetmore Order* (based on evolutionary characteristics) as detailed in *A Species List of British and Irish Birds*, BTO Guide 13, published in 1971 by The British Trust for Ornithology (see p. 261). A few exceptions in the Key to this order occur where it proved more convenient to alter the position of a species to enable comparisons on the same plate. The scientific names for the orders and families are given for each species and this will enable immediate relationships to be appreciated.

Explanation of Terms and Symbols

♂   male

♀   female

ad or **adult**   bird in its final fully developed plumage

area   section of the region covered by the book

blaze   prominent patch of colouring at base of bill

breeding plumage   plumage acquired during the breeding season

colonial   the gathering together of birds, usually of the same species, for a specific purpose such as breeding or roosting

crepuscular   active at dawn and dusk

display   active posturing, most frequent during breeding season

disyllabic   a bird's call consisting of two notes

diurnal   active during daylight

drum   activity, specific to woodpeckers, of hammering on dead or hollow wood to create far-carrying sounds

eclipse   plumage of male ducks, when closely resemble females, acquired after breeding and before full winter plumage

escapee   bird at one time confined in captivity

facial disc   specific to owls: the somewhat circular head markings creating the effect of a face

feral   populations now living and breeding in the wild, which originated from domestic or captive birds

flycatching   feeding activity of leaving perch to catch flying insects

glide   direct forward flight without movement of the wings

gregarious   gathering into flocks, often with other species

hawking   feeding activity of catching flying insects without settling

hovering   using wings and tail to remain stationary in the air

imm or **immature**   bird in a non-adult plumage

introduced   population that originates from captive birds being deliberately released in the area

juvenile   bird in the plumage with which it left the nest

larder specific to shrikes, where food is kept for later consumption by impaling on thorn bushes, wire fences, etc.

marine inhabiting sea-water areas

migrant bird not remaining in area throughout the year

mob aggressive behaviour, usually by a collection of smaller birds, towards a bird of prey or owl

monosyllabic a bird's call consisting of a single note

nocturnal active during hours of darkness

non-breeder present but not nesting in an area during the breeding season

oceanic inhabiting open oceans

oiled having plumage contaminated with oil

passage migrant bird in the process of moving from one geographical area to another

phase distinct plumage variation with no relationship to geographical range

polygamous more than one female to each male

quartering hunting by flying low over ground

race distinct plumage variation in relation to geographical range

region that part of north-west Europe covered by the Key

resident present throughout the year

soar fly with minimal movement of wings, usually in circular pattern, making use of rising air currents

speculum specific to ducks: area of often highly coloured feathers on secondaries

spinning specific to phalaropes: rapid circular movement by swimming bird to bring food to surface

sub-ad or **sub-adult** bird in nearly adult plumage

summer plumage plumage used for breeding

summer visitor bird present in summer months only

trisyllabic a bird's call consisting of three notes

up-end feeding method of water birds when body held in vertical position, fore-part below water, hind-part above water

wattles fleshy protuberances on head, particularly on game birds

web-footed having fleshy membranes between the toes

winter plumage plumage acquired outside breeding season

winter visitor bird present in winter months only

Parts of a Bird

UPPER SIDE

UNDER SIDE

1 outer tail feathers
2 upper tail coverts
3 rump
4 back (mantle)
5 nape
6 crown
7 forehead
8 upper mandible
9 lower mandible
10 chin
11 throat
12 breast
13 belly
14 flanks
15 under tail coverts
16 scapulars
17 tarsus
18 primaries
19 primary coverts
20 secondaries
   (speculum in ducks)
21 secondary coverts
22 median coverts
23 lesser coverts

24 alula (bastard wing)
25 crown stripe
26 superciliary stripe
27 eye-ring
28 eye stripe
29 lore
30 moustachial stripe
31 ear coverts
32 under wing coverts (wing linings)
33 axillaries

Note Wing-bars are formed by contrasting coloured tips to one or more of the upper wing-feather tracts.

11

Measurements

Each plate is drawn to scale, apart from insets within the white borders which are out of scale with the main plates. The plates are accompanied by a scale representing 15 cm (6 in.).

The text for each species commences with the bird's length in centimetres and inches to give some indication of size. This measurement is made from the tip of the tail to the tip of the bill when the bird is lying flat on its back and may bear no relationship with its appearance in the field if seen in flight (perhaps with trailing legs) or hunched up (as in cold weather). *These measurements should only be used as an approximate guide.*

APPARENT SIZE

ORNITHOLOGICAL MEASUREMENT

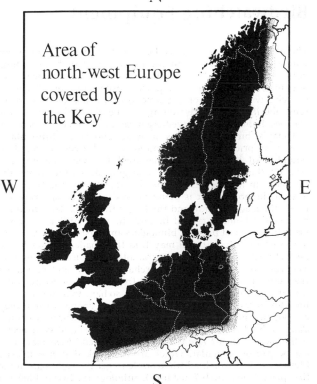

N

W   E

S

Area of
north-west Europe
covered by
the Key

Birds occurring regularly, either as residents, summer or winter
visitors, or birds of passage in any of the following countries,
are described and illustrated in the Key:

British Isles and Irish Republic   Netherlands   Denmark
France (north only)   Luxembourg   Norway
Belgium   Germany   Sweden

The northern and western limits of the area covered are easily
defined by the oceanic sea-board. The southern limit is an
imaginary line from the mouth of the Gironde River (France) to
the junction of the French, Swiss and German frontiers near
Basle. The limit of our area then follows the German borders
with Switzerland, Austria, Czechoslovakia and Poland to the
southern Baltic; and from here northwards (excluding Finland)
to the North Cape (Norway).

Birdwatching Equipment

The following notes can only be used as a guide to equipment which may prove useful in the pursuit of your birdwatching hobby. You may find that a particular piece of equipment does not suit your needs, or your pocket, especially now that there is such a wide variety of instruments on the market. It is worth remembering that birdwatching can be classed as one of the cheapest hobbies, but conversely it can be extremely expensive.

Today's birdwatcher has a wide choice of **binoculars**, ranging in price from a few pounds to well over one hundred pounds. All binoculars are classified by two numbers (e.g. 10×50), the first of which is the magnification, the second diameter, in millimetres, of the the object lens (the large lens nearest the object that is being viewed). In general terms, the larger the magnification and the larger the object lens, then the heavier the binoculars will be and the more difficult to hold. Probably the most popular binoculars amongst birdwatchers are 9×35 or 10×50, but you may find the smaller, lighter 8×30 perfectly suitable for your general all-round birdwatching use. Try your binoculars before purchasing them, and remember that looking down the high street from a shop doorway is not the same as watching birds in the field, so have them on approval for a few days' trial and do not be afraid to change them if they are not suitable for your needs. Are they comfortable to hold? Can you hold them steady? Are they heavy round your neck? Is the picture clear? Are the colours distorted? Remember that a good pair of binoculars which are well looked after will last a lifetime, so it is worth a little trouble to get the right pair in the first place. The British Trust for Ornithology (p. 261) publishes a useful guide to optical equipment which will provide you with much helpful information when you come to choose a pair of binoculars.

Many enthusiastic birdwatchers are never to be seen without their **telescopes**, and there are certain advantages to these instruments, particularly the high magnification (usually $30 \times -60 \times$) which makes it possible to study individual birds in great detail or to observe flocks more accurately over a greater distance. However, there are also disadvantages: telescopes are heavy and cumbersome to use; some form of rest is needed, and as only one eye is used, it can be extremely tiring. The acquisition of a telescope should be of secondary importance to binoculars.

As your interest in birdwatching develops, you may desire to indulge in bird photography and consequently wish to purchase a **camera**. Bird photography is a hobby in itself, and there are numerous excellent books on the subject. If you feel your interest could well develop along these lines, a good starting point is to record by means of a photograph the habitats the birds use, or sites where you have seen birds of special interest.

This will not require expensive equipment and can be done with any of the readily available 'snap-shot' type cameras. As time passes you may find that you would like to progress to a single-lens reflex, 35 mm camera with interchangeable lenses. This will provide a useful basis should bird photography grow to be your major interest.

You should have a **notebook** available to record your observations. You will find it very useful when you come to identify your birds if you have jotted down the salient characters: what the bird looked like, the presence of distinctive marks or features, shape and size of bill and legs, how it was behaving and flying. Remember that when and where you saw the bird can also help with identification. Is it found in this country, at this time of the year, in this type of habitat? On p. 240 of this book you will find a check list where you can record the species you have seen, and where and when you first saw them; but as your interest develops you may wish to record observations of interesting behaviour, nesting, feeding, etc.; this is when your notebook becomes truly important.

When out for a day's birdwatching, it is, of course, sensible to wear **suitable clothing**. This means avoid bright colours: subdued browns, greens and greys are probably best; and wear comfortable clothes, with a good selection of pockets so as to keep your hands free for the important task of holding the binoculars. A light-weight back-pack for such items as sandwiches, drinks and waterproofs is extremely useful. Some form of light-weight waterproof clothing is probably a wise precaution if birdwatching in Britain, especially if far from base. Foot-wear is equally important, for nothing is more uncomfortable than ill-fitting boots or spending the day with wet feet. Choose foot-wear suitable for the terrain, e.g. Wellingtons, walking boots, or plimsolls, but make sure they fit snuggly. For the little extra weight that you will have to carry, a spare pair of socks in the back-pack can avoid some uncomfortable hours.

DIVERS (GAVIIFORMES; GAVIIDAE) *Large water birds, mainly marine in winter, breeding on freshwater lakes. Long bodied with legs at rear, dagger-like bills. Active swimmers, diving from surface with small upward leap. Clumsy on land. Flying with typical hunchback shape and pointed wings, no gliding. Sexes alike, distinctive summer plumage, species similar in winter.*

Black-throated Diver *Gavia arctica*: 64 cm (25″) Breeds Scandinavia and northern Scotland, wintering in coastal waters throughout region, but scarce off Ireland. Breeding lakes usually deeper and larger than for RED-THROATED. **Bill not heavy** as GREAT NORTHERN and head less angular. In flight wing-beats tend to be shallower than other species. Voice: wailing breeding cry and barking flight note.

Great Northern Diver *Gavia immer*: 77 cm (30″) Winter visitor to coastal waters throughout region, small numbers summering northern Scotland. Distinctive **stout, straight bill**; peaked forehead and broad body. Flight appears heavier than other species, rather goose-like with projecting feet obvious. Takes flight with more difficulty than other divers and landings on water accompanied by much splashing. Voice: similar to Black-throated but includes loud laughing cry.

White-billed Diver *Gavia adamsii*: 91 cm (36″) Winter visitor to north Scandinavian coast. The largest diver, with **pale upturned bill** (some GREAT NORTHERNS have paler bills in winter, but ridge along upper mandible always dark). Behaviour and voice similar to Great Northern.

Red-throated Diver *Gavia stellata*: 55 cm (22″) Breeds Scandinavia, northern Ireland and northern Scotland, wintering in coastal waters throughout region but more regularly inland than other species. When breeding found on quite small lakes. Commonest and smallest diver of the region, often in small parties. Appearance generally grey and comparatively slim with **bill upturned** but can look straight. Voice: repeated quacking note.

Winter plumages of divers (Use in conjunction with size and shape.)

Black-throated: dark cap extends to lower edge of eye and base of bill, head paler than back. No white in dark feathers of head and neck. Mantle uniform in adults, some pale edgings in young birds.

Great Northern: head appears darker than back, dingy sides to upper breast, mantle can appear barred.

White-billed: as GREAT NORTHERN, but note bill shape and colour.

Red-throated: dark cap does not extend round eye and rarely reaches base of bill. Some white in dark feathers of head and neck. Dark cap narrows on hind crown. Upper-parts appear spotted with white.

16

Diver in flight

Black-throated

Great Northern

White-billed

Red-throated

BLACK-THROATED DIVER

winter

summer

GREAT NORTHERN DIVER

summer

winter

WHITE-BILLED DIVER

winter

summer

RED-THROATED DIVER

summer

winter

15 cm (6 in.)

GREBES (PODICIPEDIFORMES; PODICIPITIDAE) *Freshwater birds, but some on sea in winter. Structure similar to divers (p. 16) but smaller and feet lobed not webbed. Rarely seen flying, when most show white wing flashes. Regularly dive from surface. Rarely on land where clumsy, nesting on floating vegetation. Sexes similar, summer plumage distinctive, winter plumage dark above, light below. Juveniles with striped head and neck.*

Great Crested Grebe *Podiceps cristatus*: 48 cm (19″) Resident throughout region, except Scandinavia, where only occurs in south. Common on well-vegetated lakes, reservoirs and gravel pits, more open waters in winter with many in coastal areas. Elaborate breeding display. Long neck can be laid on back when at rest. Forms small flocks in winter. Voice: varied, commonest note a harsh barking.

Red-necked Grebe *Podiceps grisegena*: 43 cm (17″) Resident in southern Scandinavia and summer visitor to eastern Germany. Winters in coastal waters of North Sea and English Channel. Prefers marshy lakes, but rare inland in winter. Shape similar to GREAT CRESTED but body and neck thicker, head rounder. Voice: drawn-out neighing call and high-pitched '*keck-keck*'.

Slavonian Grebe *Podiceps auritus*: 33 cm (13″) Breeds in a few scattered areas in Scandinavia and northern Scotland, winters from southern Scandinavia southwards, mainly in coastal waters. Largest and rarest of the dumpy, short-billed grebes. In winter, plumage similar to BLACK-NECKED but whiter appearance, **straight bill** and flatter forehead distinctive. Voice: low-pitched trilling call.

Black-necked Grebe *Podiceps nigricollis*: 30 cm (12″) Breeds from central France eastward to southern Scandinavia, but sporadic breeder in many additional areas. Locally very common, nesting colonially. Winters on both fresh and salt water in southern Britain and France. In winter, distinguished from similar SLAVONIAN by greyer appearance, **uptilted bill** and steeper forehead. Voice: commonest note a quiet '*poo-eep*'.

Little Grebe *Tachybaptus ruficollis*: 27 cm (10·5″) Resident throughout region, except Norway and Sweden where absent. Common on fresh water with vegetation and regularly on flowing water. Rarely found at marine sites. Smallest and most secretive of the grebes but flies more readily than others. Voice: bubbling note on breeding grounds.

Identifying grebes in flight
Great Crested: white on leading edge of wings and secondaries, long necked.
Red-necked: white on wing as GREAT CRESTED, neck shorter with less white.
Slavonian: white on wings confined to secondaries.
Black-necked: white on secondaries and primaries.
Little: small, round bodied, no white on wings.

GREAT CRESTED GREBE

imm

summer

winter

RED-NECKED GREBE

summer

winter

SLAVONIAN GREBE

summer

winter

BLACK-NECKED GREBE

winter

summer

summer

LITTLE GREBE

winter

15 cm (6 in.)

SHEARWATERS (PROCELLARIIFORMES; PROCELLARIIDAE)
*Long, narrow-winged oceanic birds. Fly close to waves, banking
from side to side with stiff wing-beats and glides. 'Tube nosed',
having tube-like nostrils along bill. Come to land only to breed.
Swim well and will dive from surface. Sexes, winter and summer
plumages similar.*

Cory's Shearwater *Calonectris diomedea*: 46 cm (18″) Occurs
most regularly outside breeding season in Biscay and southern
Irish Sea, but wanders into English Channel and North Sea.
Entirely marine, rarely seen from shore. Rather FULMAR-like
(p. 22), gliding more than other shearwaters, and only member
of the group to regularly soar. **Carries wings bowed**, with
tips below level of body. Heavier and broader winged than
GREAT, sometimes with narrow white patch at base of tail,
but lacks white collar and capped appearance. Rarely follows
ships, but feeds on offal around fishing boats. Voice: unlikely
to be heard in European waters.

Manx Shearwater *Puffinus puffinus*: 35 cm (14″) Breeds on
marine islands of western Britain and north-west France.
Occasional birds wander as far as west Scandinavian coast,
otherwise oceanic and absent from area in winter. Commonest
shearwater of region, with sharply **contrasting dark upper-
parts** and **white under-parts**. Very slim compared with
larger shearwaters, with hurried flight low over water. Does
not follow ships, but gathers in large flocks on sea, particularly
near breeding grounds. Western Mediterranean race (Balearic
Shearwater), which reaches English Channel in autumn,
resembles miniature CORY'S, lacking sharp demarcation
between dark upper- and white under-parts, but flight and
behaviour as Manx. Voice: very noisy on breeding grounds
at night, with wailing and cooing cries.

Great Shearwater *Puffinus gravis*: 46 cm (18″) Marine in
western waters of area during summer and autumn, rarely
seen from land. Distinctive **capped appearance**, with **white
at base of tail** (but see CORY's). Can show marked pale line
along upper-wing when moulting. Flight MANX-like, wing-
beats faster than Cory's. Feeding birds often form large flocks
and will follow ships. Voice: harsh calls from feeding birds,
otherwise silent in European waters.

Sooty Shearwater *Puffinus griseus*: 41 cm (16″) Marine
visitor to area in autumn, more frequent in coastal waters
than other shearwaters. **All-dark shearwater** with pale
line on under-wing (confusion possible with immature
ARCTIC SKUA (p. 110)). Heavier bodied and narrower winged
than GREAT, which flight action resembles, but wing-beats
faster and wings taper to point. Often in mixed parties with
Great. Voice: silent away from southern breeding grounds.

CORY'S SHEARWATER

Balearic

MANX
SHEARWATER

GREAT
SHEARWATER

SOOTY
SHEARWATER

15 cm (6 in.)

SHEARWATERS (PROCELLARIIFORMES; PROCELLARIIDAE)

Fulmar *Fulmarus glacialis*: 47 cm (18·5") Breeds on rocky coasts of British Isles and some isolated continental sites. Nests in cliff colonies, occasionally inland on buildings. Highly marine when not breeding. Occurs in two colour phases, the 'dark phase' more numerous in northern areas. **Gull-like**, but **short tail** and **thick neck**. Flies with stiff wing-flaps and much gliding, banking from side to side low over water. Soars along cliff faces. Spits oil in defence of nest. Scavenges around fishing boats. Sits high on water when swimming, running along surface to take flight. Voice: variety of low gurgling grunts and cackles.

PETRELS (PROCELLARIIFORMES; HYDROBATIDAE) *Small, dark, white-rumped oceanic birds. Rarely seen from land except when storm driven. Nest on rocky coasts and islands where highly nocturnal. Flutter low over waves, often with feet dangling, appearing to 'walk' on surface. Frequently in small flocks. 'Tube nosed', having tube-like nostrils along bill. Sexes, winter and summer plumages similar.*

Storm Petrel *Hydrobates pelagicus*: 15 cm (6") Breeds on isolated rocky coasts of western Britain and France, otherwise oceanic. Rarely seen from shore. Smallest and commonest petrel, with **square tail** and **long pointed wings**. Restricted pale wing-bar on upper-wing, only petrel with pale area on under-wing. Flight very weak and fluttering, resembling bat. Follows ships. Voice: purring call during night at nest site.

Wilson's Petrel *Oceanites oceanicus*: 18 cm (7") Scarce oceanic visitor, rarely seen from land, but sometimes common in Bay of Biscay and approaches to English Channel. Wings less pointed than other petrels, with more **gliding flight** when **feet extend beyond square tail**. Pale area on wings more extensive than STORM PETREL. Follows ships. 'Walks' on water with wings raised and tail spread. Voice: unlikely to be heard in European waters.

Leach's Petrel *Oceanodroma leucorrhoa*: 20 cm (8") Breeds on remote rocky islands of the Atlantic, otherwise oceanic, rarely seen from land. Longer winged and bodied than STORM PETREL, with **forked tail** (difficult to see in flight), **extensive pale area on wings** and less pure white rump than other petrels. Flight bounding and darting, with little 'walking' on water. Does not follow ships. Voice: churring and crooning calls from nest site during night.

FULMAR

dark
phase

light
phase

STORM PETREL

WILSON'S
PETREL

LEACH'S
PETREL

15 cm (6 in.)

GANNETS (PELECANIFORMES; SULIDAE)

Gannet *Sula bassana*: 90 cm (36") Nests in dense colonies on islands of Atlantic coast and North Sea, but occurs in all maritime localities of region. Often found far out to sea, but regularly seen from shore. Large, goose sized, with distinctive **pointed, elongated body**. Flies with rather rapid, stiff wing-beats, but glides readily, often skimming low over waves. Will soar high above sea and **dive vertically** for fish with wings half-open, folding them against body at moment of entry. Often feeds in flocks. Swims well with body high on water and tail raised. Takes flight from surface by 'running' along water. Occasionally follows ships. Sexes, winter and summer plumages similar. Immatures take five years to attain full adult plumage. Voice: harsh barking calls at breeding sites.

CORMORANTS (PELECANIFORMES; PHALACROCORACIDAE)

Large, dark sea-birds. Mainly coastal. Long bills and pointed wings. Swim readily, diving from surface (see divers, p. 16), but head held upwards when swimming and above line of body when flying. Frequently perch with wings outstretched. Nest colonially on coastal cliffs and rocks. Sexes, summer and winter plumages similar. Immatures have browner plumage with paler under-parts.

Cormorant *Phalacrocorax carbo*: 88 cm (35") Largely coastal throughout region, nesting semi-colonially on cliffs. Occasionally inland, especially in winter. Larger and heavier than SHAG, with deeper hooked bill and **white chin**, and, **in breeding plumage, white thighs**. Plumage appears black, more southern birds often with white heads and neck. Fairly rapid, direct flight, flocks often in V-formation. Immature plumage brown with whitish under-parts. Voice: guttural groaning calls at breeding site.

Shag *Phalacrocorax aristotelis*: 76 cm (30") Confined to more northern and western rocky coasts of region, where nests colonially, often mixed with CORMORANTS. Scarce elsewhere and inland. Smaller version of Cormorant with bottle-green plumage **appearing black** and **showing no white**. Crested in breeding season. Compared with Cormorant, thinner, shorter neck, with steeper forehead but smaller head. Slimmer, finer bill and wing-beats faster. Behaviour similar to Cormorant, but feeds and dives in more open water, remaining submerged for longer periods. Immatures brown, but lack the extensive white under-parts of young Cormorants. Voice: harsh rasping croak and grunting and hissing noises at breeding site.

ad

GANNET

sub-ad

imm

CORMORANT

imm

ad

ad

southern race

SHAG

imm

ad

ad summer

15 cm (6 in.)

HERONS (CICONIIFORMES; ARDEIDAE) *Large wading birds with long legs, neck and bill, frequenting shallow water. In flight, broad winged, short tailed, and legs trailing visibly. Neck curled in flight with a marked bulge. Colonial in breeding season, and gregarious at all times. Many species nest in trees. Sexes (except Little Bittern), summer and winter plumages similar, but breeding plumage often with elongated head plumes. Immatures resemble less well-marked adults.*

Grey Heron *Ardea cinerea*: 90 cm (36") but body only 40 cm (16") Found throughout region, but only in west and south of Scandinavia. Commonest, most readily seen heron of area with **large size** and **grey plumage** distinctive. Found at most freshwater sites, also on coast where more frequent in winter. Stands, often on one leg, motionless in shallow water with neck stretched or hunched, suddenly darting bill into water to catch food. Larger prey often carried to dry land for eating. Walks with slow and deliberate pace, feet lifted carefully in and out of water often accompanied with a shaking movement. Perches readily in trees, where roosts and nests in colonies. Flight slow and heavy, but will soar and glide on very broad, rounded wings which are held arched with tips pointed downwards. Frequently mobbed by communal nesting species such as rooks and gulls. Voice: most regularly heard call a distinctive '*fraaank*'.

Purple Heron *Ardea purpurea*: 80 cm (31") Summer visitor to southern areas of region. Found in swamps, marshes and reed-beds, where more secretive than GREY HERON and less inclined to perch. Smaller and darker than Grey Heron, lacking marked contrast in wing coloration and without white patches at joint on leading edge of wings. Thinner than Grey Heron with **small head** and **thin neck** which produces a deeper bulge in flight, when feet project further beyond tail. Voice: less vocal than Grey Heron, but call similar although less harsh.

Little Egret *Egretta garzetta*: 55 cm (22") Summer visitor to extreme south of region. Frequents shallow swamps and marshes, both fresh and coastal waters. Behaviour and habits typical of family. Perches in trees and bushes where roosts and breeds communally. Flight leisurely, with infrequent short glides. A distinctive small, all-white heron, with **dark bill** and legs, and **yellow feet** which can be clearly seen in flight. A rare black phase, with almost entire plumage dark, does occur. Voice: a harsh barking call at breeding grounds, otherwise silent.

GREY HERON

imm

PURPLE
HERON

imm

LITTLE
EGRET

breeding plumage

15 cm (6 in.)

HERONS (CICONIIFORMES; ARDEIDAE)

Squacco Heron *Ardeola ralloides*: 45 cm (18″) Summer
visitor to France in extreme central-southern area of region.
Inhabits marshes and swamps, but less frequently in open
than LITTLE EGRET (p. 26). Smallest white heron of region, with
thick-necked, stocky appearance. **Plumage** rather **sandy
when settled,** but **very white** when **in flight** on short, broad,
rounded wings. Perches freely in trees, where nests colonially,
often with other species. Largely crepuscular, but can be
highly active throughout day. Voice: high-pitched croak,
most vocal at dusk and dawn.

Night Heron *Nycticorax nycticorax*: 60 cm (24″) Summer
visitor to south of region and Holland. Feral population at
Edinburgh zoo results in several British records. Found in
densely vegetated swamps and marshes, occasionally in dry
areas or salt marshes. Freely perches in trees and bushes where
it roosts and nests, sometimes climbing amongst very slender
twigs. Very skulking, most active at dusk and during night,
spending day crouched in vegetation or bushes. Always
hunched in appearance, looking small, with rather shorter
legs than other herons. Broad winged and dumpy in flight,
with more rapid, deliberate wing-beats than other herons,
and frequent long glides with wings held horizontal. **Adult**
appears **black and white,** **immature** somewhat like small
BITTERN but **large white spots on wings.** Voice: harsh croak.

Little Bittern *Ixobrychus minutus*: 35 cm (14″) Summer
visitor south of English Channel and North Sea. **Smallest
member of family** in area, found in dense vegetation by
fresh water, particularly reed-beds where will climb amongst
stems. Very skulking and secretive, rarely seen except when
flushed, preferring to run rather than fly when disturbed.
Largely crepuscular; not colonial. When alarmed, 'freezes'
in upright position like BITTERN. Rapid wing-beats and long
glides **in flight**, when **contrasting pale areas of wings**
very conspicuous. Immature resembles female. Voice: very
frog-like series of croaks and grunts, and deep *'thump'*
repeated at regular intervals.

Bittern *Botaurus stellaris*: 75 cm (30″)   Resident from southern
Scandinavia and England southwards. Largely confined
to extensive reed-beds but found in other freshwater sites
during severe weather. Very skulking, well camouflaged
with **mottled plumage** and rarely seen except when flies;
not colonial and rarely perches in trees. 'Freezes' when
alarmed with head stretched upwards, contrasting with
normal crouching posture. Slow heron-like flight (p. 26),
usually low over reeds, with rather rounded appearance.
Voice: very vocal on breeding grounds; distinctive booming
call, rather like distant fog-horn, from January–June. Harsh
barking flight note.

SQUACCO HERON

breeding plumage

imm

imm

ad

NIGHT HERON

ad

♀ & imm

LITTLE BITTERN

♂

BITTERN

freeze posture

15 cm (6 in.)

STORKS (CICONIIFORMES; CICONIIDAE) *Large, long-necked, long-legged, long-billed wading birds of damp or grassy areas. Legs and stout bill red. Plumage black and white. Flight with neck outstretched (unlike herons) and legs trailing beyond short tail. Nest on trees and roofs. Sexes, summer and winter plumages similar. Juveniles resemble adults with duller bills and legs.*

White Stork *Ciconia ciconia*: 105 cm (40") Breeds in Germany, Netherlands and southern Scandinavia, migrating south of Europe in winter. Decreasing in western Europe. Inhabits farmland and open grassy areas, nesting on buildings. Rather tame and approachable near nesting grounds, frequently found feeding amongst farm workers, often by roadside. Away from breeding grounds, more shy. Slow and deliberate walk, often standing or perched on one leg. **White plumage** with **black wings** distinctive. Occurs in loose scattered flocks. Flight slow, much gliding, with extended neck and legs slightly drooped below line of body. Sometimes soars in flocks, and parties on migration will fly in V-formation. Voice: usually silent, but hisses and makes clattering noise with bill at nest site.

Black Stork *Ciconia nigra*: 100 cm (39") Occurs as summer visitor in eastern Germany. Found in more wooded sites than WHITE STORK, where nests in trees, usually at a considerable height. Inhabits more open country when on migration. Size, structure, flight and actions similar to White Stork, but basic differences of **black plumage** and **white belly** help to avoid confusion. More solitary and shy than White Stork, rarely seen in more than ones or twos. Immatures are browner, lacking plumage gloss of adults. Voice: more vocal than White Stork with range of 'sawing' and musical notes. Bill clattering less frequent.

SPOONBILLS (CICONIIFORMES; THRESKIORNITHIDAE)

Spoonbill *Platalea leucorodia*: 85 cm (34") Summer visitor to isolated breeding sites in Netherlands. Infrequent elsewhere in area as migrant or rare winter visitor. Found in shallow-water areas, both coastal and inland, nesting colonially in reed-beds, or sometimes in trees. Sociable, but rarely in flocks mixed with other species. Bird's structure and movements on ground very heron-like (p. 26), but with shorter, thicker neck. **White plumage**, **spatulate bill shape** distinctive, and bill looks slightly decurved from side view. Frequently stands on one leg. Feeds by sweeping bill from side to side in water, generally with more active feeding at dusk. Flies with outstretched, slightly sagging neck and trailing legs. Flight slow, with steady wing-beats, much gliding and some soaring. Parties usually fly in extended line. Sexes similar, crested in breeding plumage. Immatures have black wing-tips and pale bill. Voice: usually silent, but occasional grunt-like calls.

WHITE STORK

ad

imm

BLACK STORK

ad

imm

ad

SPOONBILL

imm

ad summer

15 cm (6 in.)

DUCKS, GEESE and SWANS (ANSERIFORMES; ANATIDAE)
Swimming, web-footed water birds. Longish neck, short legs, narrow pointed wings and usually with flat, blunt bills. Most nest on ground; young active, swimming and walking within a few hours of hatching. The family may be divided into the following groups: **Surface-feeding ducks** *Feed by dabbling in shallow water, or up-ending. When standing, body held parallel to ground. Take flight from water by jumping into air. Both sexes have bright coloured patch on secondaries (speculum). Sexes different, immatures and males in late summer (eclipse) resemble females.* **Diving ducks** *Feed by diving from surface. Stand with body in near vertical position. Run along surface of water to take flight. Have wing-bars and markings (no speculum). Sexes different, immatures resemble females.* **Shelducks** *Large, black-and-white, goose-like ducks. Sexes similar.* **Eiders** *Large, diving sea ducks with heavy triangular bills. Males strikingly black and white, females brown.* **Stifftails** *Small, dumpy diving ducks with cocked-up tail.* **Sawbills** *Slim, long necked, slender billed and crested. Dive for animal food. Appearance on water diver-like (p. 16). Run along surface to take flight. Rarely seen out of water. Sexes different, immatures resemble females.* **Geese** *Large and noisy, bulkier than ducks, less active flight. Mainly feed by grazing. Sociable when not breeding, flying in V-formation. Sexes and immatures similar.* **Swans** *Largest all-white waterfowl. Sexes similar, immatures ash-brown.*

SURFACE-FEEDING DUCKS (ANSERIFORMES; ANATIDAE)

Mallard *Anas platyrhynchos*: 58 cm (23″)   Found throughout region, but absent from northern Scandinavia in winter. **Commonest dabbling duck** of the area, breeding on almost any fresh water (flowing or stagnant) from town ponds to reservoirs and marshes. Found on river estuaries and coastal sites in winter. Wild ancestor of farmyard ducks – note curled upper tail feathers of males. Frequently hybridizes with 'escaped' farm ducks, resulting in many strangely marked individuals. Sits lower on water than most dabbling ducks (larger and heavier), and will perch on partially submerged trees and rocks. Flight rapid, wing-beats shallow. Males flock while females tend nest and young. Voice: female has loud quack; male, a softer 'kweek'.

Gadwall *Anas strepera*: 50 cm (20″)   Breeds at scattered sites from southern Scandinavia westwards; otherwise winter visitor or migrant throughout region, except Scandinavia. More local than MALLARD, rarely found in marine sites. Appearance similar to rather small female Mallard, but note **greyness** and **black under-tail of male**, and **white speculum** (especially when in flight). Forehead less rounded than Mallard. Habits much as Mallard, but shyer and rarely in large groups. Wing-beats more rapid and wings more pointed. Voice: female has very soft Mallard-like quack; male, a rather nasal croaking note.

♂

eclipse ♂

imm ♂

♀

MALLARD

♀ ♂

♀

GADWALL

imm ♂

♂

eclipse ♂

♂

♀

15 cm (6 in.)

SURFACE-FEEDING DUCKS (ANSERIFORMES; ANATIDAE)

Teal *Anas crecca*: 32 cm (13″) Found throughout region all year, except Scandinavia where summer visitor in north. Breeds at freshwater sites with dense vegetation, the nest often some way from open water. Winters on larger water areas including coastal localities. **Smallest of the dabbling ducks**, shy when breeding, but forming compact flocks in winter. Very agile, rapid flight, flocks springing from water and wheeling and diving through air rather like some shore waders. North American race, Green-winged Teal, occasionally occurs in western Europe, but only males are distinguishable. Females resemble female GARGANEY, but differ by rounder forehead, finer bill, less distinct facial markings, darker throat, and in flight by darker speculum and lack of black leading edge to under-wing. Voice: male has distinctive '*kriick kriick*' call; female, a quiet nasal quack.

Garganey *Anas querquedula*: 38 cm (15″) Summer visitor to region, north to central Britain and southern Sweden. Habitat similar to TEAL, but mainly low-lying areas and rarely on salt water. Only slightly larger than Teal, but male distinctive; (for differences between the females see Teal). Rarely in large flocks; after breeding small numbers frequently join Teal flocks. Habits similar to Teal, but rapid flight less erratic, more SHOVELER-like (p. 36). Voice: male has distinctive rattling, crackling sound; female, a low-pitched quack.

Wigeon *Anas penelope*: 45 cm (18″) Breeds in Scandinavia and northern Britain at freshwater sites in upland or tundra areas. Winters from southern Scandinavia southward on large areas of water including reservoirs and coastal sites. A distinctively shaped duck with **small bill**, **short neck**, peaked forehead and pointed tail. Often in large flocks in winter, rarely mixed with other species, and frequently grazing on fields or mud-flats, where walks and runs with ease. Flight fast, in compact flocks with deeper wing-strokes than most duck. Voice: distinctive '*whee-oo*' whistle of male; female has weak purring call.

Pintail *Anas acuta*: 56 cm (22″), plus 10 cm (4″) tail in male. Breeds in Scandinavia and Germany, with isolated nesting elsewhere in region. Winters throughout region, except Scandinavia. Found at freshwater pools and marshes, occurring at coastal sites in winter. Drake distinctive, duck resembles WIGEON but more pointed tail, longer and thinner neck and narrower wings. Usually in pairs or small flocks, rather shy but mixes with other species. Voice: male has short, low whistling call; female, a hoarse low quack.

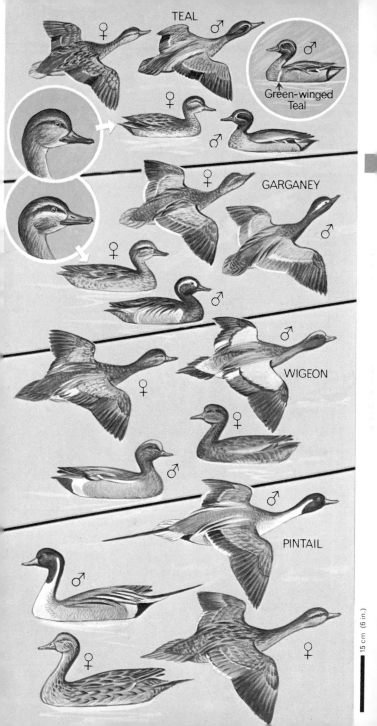

TEAL

Green-winged
Teal

GARGANEY

WIGEON

PINTAIL

15 cm (6 in.)

SURFACE-FEEDING DUCKS (ANSERIFORMES; ANATIDAE)

Shoveler *Anas clypeata*: 50 cm (20″)   Breeding in region from southern Scandinavia westwards, wintering from Holland westwards. Found on lowland water areas with extensive shallows and vegetation, more open water and coastal in winter. Characteristic **broad, flat bill** distinguishes species, on water appearing very low fronted with head down, stocky appearance and short neck. In flight heavy bill gives appearance of wings far back on body. Wing-beats rapid with twists and turns in flight but less agile than TEAL (p. 34), with which occasionally mixes, but small flocks usually separate. Frequently rests on water's edge, but rarely walks as feet and legs small and weak compared with other surface feeders. Only occasionally up-ends, feeds actively by rapidly sifting mud and water through bill. Voice: male has double *'chook chook'* note; female, a soft Mallard-like quack.

Mandarin Duck *Aix galericulata*: 43 cm (17″)   An introduced Asiatic species now living wild in British Isles and a few isolated Continental areas, but frequently escapes from wildfowl collections. Prefers freshwater sites surrounded by woodlands where freely perches amongst trees and nests in holes. Both sexes unlike other European ducks, but female similar to female North American Carolina or Wood Duck, *Aix sponsa*, another escapee from collections. Best distinguished by long white line extending behind eye-ring, less extensive white chin and throat and lack of greenish hue to crown. In flight the **short neck** and rather long **wedge-shaped tail** give characteristic outline. Rarely feeds in water, mainly on ground amongst trees but will visit stubble fields. Voice: most vocal in flight when utters a sharp whistling call.

DIVING DUCKS (ANSERIFORMES; ANATIDAE)

Red-crested Pochard *Netta rufina*: 56 cm (22″)   Occurs as breeding species in north Germany, Denmark and Holland, but rather scattered and irregular elsewhere. Often escapes from waterfowl collections. Inhabits lagoons and marshes with surrounding reeds, usually coastal. Distinctive, although wary, diving duck which also feeds by up-ending in shallower water. Rarely in large flocks, frequently mixing with other species. Characteristic **thin bill** and male can raise crest feathers to give large-headed appearance. Female can be mistaken for grebe in winter plumage (p. 18) or female COMMON SCOTER (p. 42) which have similar facial patterns, but sits higher on water often with head bent forward and generally placid movements. Rather heavily built, rising from water with run and whirring wings when red legs can be seen and appearing as large or larger than MALLARD (p. 32) in flight. Comes to land more frequently than other diving ducks, where body is held more horizontally and walks with less difficulty. Voice: generally silent except on breeding grounds, flight note a grating, rattle-like *'kurrr'*.

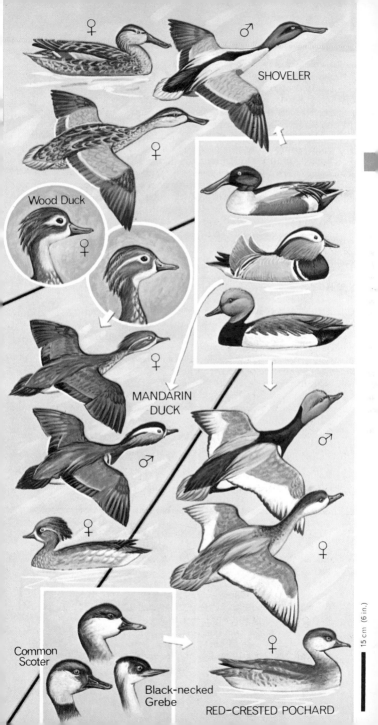

♀

♂

SHOVELER

♀

Wood Duck

♀

♀

MANDARIN
DUCK

♂

♀

♂

♀

Common
Scoter

Black-necked
Grebe

♀

RED-CRESTED POCHARD

15 cm (6 in.)

DIVING DUCKS (ANSERIFORMES; ANATIDAE)

Scaup *Aythya marila*: 48 cm (19″)   Breeds on freshwater lakes of Norway and Sweden (except extreme south), wintering in coastal areas of North Sea, English Channel and British Isles. Particularly fond of estuaries in winter months, and rarely seen inland apart from occasional females or young birds. The male is easily distinguished from similar TUFTED by **grey back**, but identification of females and isolated young or moulting birds can be difficult. Larger and broader than Tufted, with rounder **head lacking all signs of tuft**. Bill broader, base of female's is surrounded by prominent white blaze, more extensive than occasional white on Tufted. Blaze virtually lost in breeding season, but pale cheeks acquired. Eclipse male lacks clear-cut, white, round bill, otherwise resembles female with greyish back. Dives readily, even on very rough seas, where frequently mixes with eider (p. 44) or scoter (p. 42). Often flies or sits on water in spread line rather than compact flock. Voice: silent in winter, but some calling on breeding grounds.

Tufted Duck *Aythya fuligula*: 43 cm (17″)   Found throughout region all year except much of Scandinavia in winter. Occurs on freshwater sites with vegetation in breeding season, some moving to more open water in winter. Rare on salt water. **Commonest diving duck** of region, becoming tame on town or park ponds. Only water-fowl with **drooping crest**, less distinct in the all-brown female which sometimes has white at base of bill (see SCAUP) or under tail (see FERRUGINOUS, p. 40). Male in eclipse resembles rather dark female. As with all diving ducks, much time spent preening, when on water rolling on side to preen under-parts. Usually in small parties, often mixed with POCHARD, but when in larger flocks flight is often in formation ('V' or extended line). Feeding parties frequently follow one another, diving from surface in quick succession. Voice: grating flight call and whistling note on breeding grounds.

Pochard *Aythya ferina*: 46 cm (18″)   Summer visitor to southern Scandinavia, winter visitor to western Britain and western France, resident elsewhere in region. Habitat as TUFTED, but found on some salt-water sites. Both sexes **lack prominent white wing-bars** of other diving ducks; male in eclipse resembling female with greyer back. Habits similar to Tufted but rarely feeds in such deep water and more active morning and evening, resting during the day. Sometimes sits on water's edge, but rarely comes to land; prefers resting on water where swims with low body and tail trailing in water. Voice: a variety of whistling, groaning calls, particularly in flight.

SCAUP

eclipse

♂

♀

summer ♀

♀

winter

♂

♀

♂

♀

TUFTED DUCK

♂

♂

♀

POCHARD

♀

preening

15 cm (6 in.)

DIVING DUCKS (ANSERIFORMES; ANATIDAE)

Ferruginous Duck *Aythya nyroca*: 40 cm (16″) Winters from central France eastwards, with a few isolated breeding localities within this area. Regular escapee from waterfowl collections. Frequents reed-beds and other freshwater sites with dense vegetation. Rare on salt water. A small, skulking, although active diving duck, not unlike female TUFTED (p. 38), but with distinctive **high-domed head** and **white under-tail** (but see Tufted). In flight, white wing-bar slightly longer and more curved than in related species. Sits higher on water than other diving ducks, with tail held high. Rarely mixes with other species, except POCHARD (p. 38), favouring the shallower water for diving where will occasionally up-end. Voice: harsh grating flight note.

Goldeneye *Bucephala clangula*: 45 cm (18″) Summers in Scandinavia, except extreme south; wintering throughout remainder of region. Frequents freshwater sites in woodlands, where nests in suitable holes in trees (such as those left by woodpeckers) or in banks. On fresh and salt water in winter. Both sexes have distinctive **peaked head**, almost triangular in shape, with short bill. Rarely on land, and takes flight with more ease than other diving ducks. In flight, short wings have distinctive whistling note, and bird looks **stout bodied** and **short necked**. Found in large flocks in a few localities, but usually small parties or singles, rarely mixing with other species. Seldom comes to land, but very active diver, small parties often diving in unison. In late winter and spring male has characteristic display with head thrown back and bill pointing skywards. Voice: usually silent, but male has harsh nasal note in spring.

Long-tailed Duck *Clangula hyemalis*: 40 cm (16″) plus 12 cm (5″) tail in adult males. Breeds in tundra localities of northern Scandinavia, wintering in coastal sites north of English Channel. Scarce inland. A small diving sea duck, **lacking any wing pattern**, with very small bill and distinctive seasonal plumage. Rare on land, often found well out to sea, where highly gregarious but seldom with other species. Swims low but buoyantly and active even in very rough seas. Often tame. Fast, swinging flight action, curved wings not raised above level of body. Drops on to water when settling, rather than gliding down. Voice: male noisy on breeding grounds with series of howling notes. Female has quiet quack. Flocks at sea sometimes very vocal.

FERRUGINOUS DUCK

♂ ♀

♂ ♀

GOLDENEYE

♀ ♂

♀ ♂

imm

eclipse ♂

LONG-TAILED DUCK

winter ♂

♀ winter

♂ summer

♀ summer

imm ♂

15 cm (6 in.)

DIVING DUCKS (ANSERIFORMES; ANATIDAE)

Velvet Scoter *Melanitta fusca*: 55 cm (22″)   Breeds on fresh-water sites and some off-shore islands in northern Scandinavia, wintering in coastal areas of Norway, North Sea, English Channel and France. Rarer inland than COMMON SCOTER and more frequent on exposed waters. Usually winters in small compact flocks, feeding and diving in unison, but occasionally mixed with Common Scoter and eider (p. 44). Distinguished from smaller Common Scoter by **white wing-patch**, most obvious in flight, but usually partially visible when at rest. Red feet noticeable when submerges with half-opened wings. Takes flight with difficulty, looking heavy headed and thick necked. Young resemble female. Voice: not very vocal; usual call a growling whistle.

Common Scoter *Melanitta nigra*: 48 cm (19″)   Breeds at freshwater sites in northern Scandinavia, Scotland and Ireland, wintering mainly in coastal areas throughout region. Some non-breeding birds remain in wintering areas through-out summer. **Male** is **all black, female brown** with paler face-pattern as RED-CRESTED POCHARD (p. 36). Young resemble female. Often winters in large flocks, usually in more sheltered waters than VELVET SCOTER. When migrating or changing feeding grounds, compact flocks fly low over sea, frequently changing shape to extended line or V-formation. Rarely comes to land except when oiled or storm driven. Swims buoyantly with neck sunk between shoulders and pointed tail cocked; when alarmed submerges body and straightens neck. Voice: variety of growling and cooing notes.

SHELDUCKS (ANSERIFORMES; ANATIDAE)

Shelduck *Tadorna tadorna*: 60 cm (24″)   Mainly coastal throughout region except absent northernmost Scandinavia and winter visitor to Atlantic coast of France. Large, late summer moulting concentrations on German coast. Nests in burrows. Large, rather goose-like duck with **striking black-and-white plumage**. Male in eclipse resembles female. Regularly on land, where walks with ease, feeding in shallows, estuary mud, etc. Takes flight with ease, when goose-like with slow wing-beats. Unfledged young often in large groups of several broods, diving regularly and with ease when alarmed. Voice: variety of deep nasal notes; male has whistling flight call.

VELVET SCOTER

COMMON SCOTER

SHELDUCK

imm

15 cm (6 in.)

EIDERS (ANSERIFORMES; ANATIDAE)

Steller's Eider *Polysticta stelleri*: 45 cm (18")   Found only on the north coast of Norway in winter, where frequently close in shore and can be very tame. Smaller, more compact than other eiders, with distinctive head and bill shape. Dives with partially opened wings, but will up-end in shallow water. When swimming, rather long pointed tail held slightly upwards. Takes off from water as easily as surface feeder, with flight action faster than other eiders. Male in eclipse resembles female, apart from wing patterning; young resemble female. Young males slowly acquire adult plumage during first twelve months. Voice: whistling note in flight; male has crooning call; female, a harsh quack.

Eider *Somateria mollissima*: 59 cm (23")   Coastal throughout region, nesting in all areas except southern Britain and France, where winter visitor and non-breeders summer. Rarely found on fresh water or inland. **Commonest of the eiders**. Very tame on breeding grounds, often nests far from water, birds walking to and from site with typical slow rolling movement. Frequently leaves water to rest on suitable coast. Size and shape distinctive; adult male unmistakable, female has flatter head than KING EIDER, with continuous line from crown to tip of bill. Young resemble female, but young and eclipse males show wide variety of plumage, young developing adult plumage by stages during first two years, perhaps longer. When swimming, tail held along water, with long run required to take flight. Flight action heavy with head held rather low on short thick neck. Flocks usually fly low over sea in extended line, where presence of adult males makes identification simple. Voice: male has crooning call on breeding grounds; female, a grating note.

King Eider *Somateria spectabilis*: 56 cm (22")   Winters on coast of northern Norway. Male is unmistakable, female rather more rufous than EIDER with different head shape. Young resemble female, young males showing wide variety of plumage before reaching full adult dress, but never with white on back. Flight and habits resemble Eider with which often mixes, but tends to feed in deeper water. Voice: typical call a cooing note.

STELLER'S EIDER

♀

eclipse ♂

♂

♂

EIDER

♀

♂

imm ♂

moulting ♂

♀

♂

imm ♂

eclipse ♂

KING EIDER

15 cm (6 in.)

STIFFTAILS (ANSERIFORMES; ANATIDAE)

Ruddy Duck *Oxyura jamaicensis*: 40 cm (16") North American species, regularly kept in waterfowl collections with established feral population in western England. Prefers shallow, well-vegetated freshwater pools, occurring on more open water in winter. **Squat, short-necked** diving duck, regularly **swimming with tail cocked**. When alarmed can sink below surface with only head visible. In flight, rather short rounded wings produce fast action with rapid wing-beats giving whirring or buzzing effect. Eclipse males resemble females but retain white cheeks. Voice: generally silent, but males have variety of notes during courtship.

SAWBILLS (ANSERIFORMES; ANATIDAE)

Red-breasted Merganser *Mergus serrator*: 58 cm (23") Breeds in Ireland, northern Britain and Scandinavia south to north Germany, wintering in coastal areas throughout region. Rare on fresh water. A ground-nesting sawbill, more marine than other species. Rarely occurs in large concentrations, but small flocks form after breeding. A smaller, slimmer-necked bird than GOOSANDER, males distinctive, females similar, but crest higher on head and white of chin continues on to breast. Upper-parts more brownish. Frequently swims with jerking movements of head. Voice: male has rasping double call; female, a guttural note.

Goosander *Mergus merganser*: 67 cm (26") Nests in holes in trees in northern Britain and Scandinavia. Winters from southern Norway southwards, but absent from Ireland and western France. Found on forested lakes and rivers, more open water in winter and rare on salt water. Largest of the sawbills, swimming fast and low with back nearly awash. Readily swims with head below surface searching for food, diving easily and smoothly, appearing to glide beneath surface. Rather shy, taking flight with laboured run along surface. Has typical long, thin sawbill shape in flight. Rarely in large flocks, small groups often mingling with other ducks. Compared with RED-BREASTED MERGANSER, female has drooping crest, more blue-grey back and sharply demarked throat-band. Eclipse male resembles female but retains wing patterning. Voice: male usually silent; female has guttural call.

Smew *Mergus albellus*: 40 cm (16") Nests in tree holes in northern Norway, wintering from southern Scandinavia and England southwards. Found on inland lakes in forested areas, more open water in winter. Smallest of the sawbills, with very small bill. Swims high on water and can spring into air from surface. Parties often mix with other ducks. Females resemble grebes (p. 18). Voice: usually silent, male has whistling note.

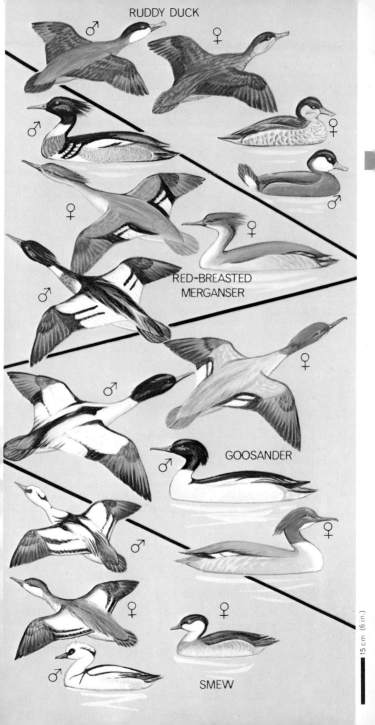

RUDDY DUCK

♂ ♀

♀

♂

♂

♀

♀

RED-BREASTED
MERGANSER

♀

♂

GOOSANDER

♂

♀

♂

♀

♀

SMEW

15 cm (6 in.)

GEESE (ANSERIFORMES; ANATIDAE)

Greylag Goose *Anser anser*: 75–90 cm (30–35″) Breeds in lowland areas of coastal Scandinavia and Scotland; introduced birds now widely resident in Britain on a variety of water areas. Winters from North Sea coasts west to Ireland, favouring marshes and wide variety of farmland. The largest of the grey geese, with **large prominent bill** lacking any dark at base, and with **striking grey forewings** very obvious in flight (but see PINK-FOOTED GOOSE, p. 50). Walks and flies heavily, taking flight from land with ease, but with more difficulty from water, when flaps along surface. Highly gregarious, even breeding in loose colonies, with flocks flighting to and from feeding grounds in line or V-formation. Flocks coming in to land can perform striking aerial evolutions. Apart from introduced birds, generally shy and unapproachable. Eastern race (rare in western Europe) has pink bill. Voice: resembles farmyard goose (domestic descendant of species) including typical hissing note.

White-fronted Goose *Anser albifrons*: 65–75 cm (25–30″) Siberian visitor to region, wintering from northern Germany to Biscay and British Isles. Birds from Greenland winter in Ireland and western Scotland. Found on coastal marshes and farmland, unusual on stubble or crops. Adults are most distinctive of grey geese with **barred under-parts** and **white forehead**, but young lack these markings. Behaviour as GREYLAG but wing-beats faster and flight more active, taking off vertically from ground. In flight looks smaller headed and thinner necked. Highly gregarious, winter flocks numbering several hundred in favoured areas. The Greenland race has yellow bill. Voice: laughing quality, resembling calls from distant dog pack.

Lesser White-fronted Goose *Anser erythropus*: 50–65 cm (20–25″) Breeds in northern Scandinavia. Rare in remainder of region, occasional individuals mingling with WHITE-FRONTED flocks. Nests inland on dry tundra, wintering on coastal marshes. Smallest of the grey geese, often consorting with other species. Easily overlooked amongst White-fronted flock but differs in being smaller, slightly darker, with yellow eye-ring, more extensive **white on forehead reaching to crown**, smaller and shorter pink bill, and closed wings extending beyond tail of standing bird. Crops grass with faster feeding rate than White-fronted, and wing-beats more rapid in flight, otherwise behaviour as White-fronted. Young birds lack white forehead and dark belly bars, but have yellow eye-ring. Voice: resembles White-fronted but more high pitched and squeaky.

48

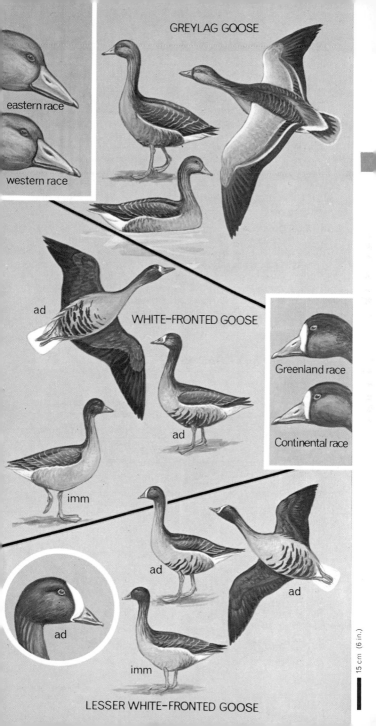

GREYLAG GOOSE

eastern race

western race

WHITE-FRONTED GOOSE

Greenland race

Continental race

ad

ad

imm

ad

imm

ad

ad

LESSER WHITE-FRONTED GOOSE

15 cm (6 in.)

GEESE (ANSERIFORMES; ANATIDAE)

Bean Goose *Anser fabalis*: 70–90 cm (28–35") Breeds at freshwater sites in central and northern Scandinavia, wintering on grassland areas south to central France. Introduced birds now resident in some areas of Britain. In size, approaches GREYLAG GOOSE (p. 48), but slimmer build with longer neck and noticeably **dark**, browner **plumage**, lacking pale grey forewings. Rather long **bill**, usually dark, **marked with orange** (tundra race), but sometimes virtually entirely orange (forest race). Behaviour similar to other grey geese, often in large flocks flighting regularly each dawn and dusk, preferring freshwater sites. Voice: less vocal than other geese, lower pitched, more honking call than Pink-footed, resembling bray of donkey.

Pink-footed Goose *Anser brachyrhynchus*: 60–75 cm (24–30") Winter visitor to region, occurring in northern and eastern Britain and coastal areas from Belgium to western Norway. Prefers arable farmland, but in coastal areas regularly flights to salt-water sites for roosting. Somewhat similar to BEAN GOOSE but markedly smaller, different leg colour, short dark **bill with pink**, and **dark head and neck contrasting with back**. In flight, pale grey of forewings extends across back (unlike larger, heavier GREYLAG, p. 48). Young birds resemble young WHITE-FRONTED (p. 48), distinguished by leg colour, rounder, smaller head, usually some dark on bill and bluer-grey back. Often in large unapproachable flocks. Habits resemble other grey geese. Voice: highly vocal, a continuous, rather shrill, two-syllable *'wink-wink'*.

Bar-headed Goose *Anser indicus*: 75 cm (30") Introduced birds now resident in Sweden, and escapees from waterfowl collections frequently appear among other geese or swans throughout region. Can be found on any water area, but favours rivers, grazing on nearby crops and grassland. Very pale goose with **strong head and neck markings**. Voice: musical double note.

Egyptian Goose *Alopochen aegyptiaca*: 70 cm (27") Introduced birds now resident in East Anglia, with escapees from waterfowl collections appearing throughout region. Frequents freshwater areas, often near wooded sites where regularly perches in trees or on submerged rocks. Rather distinctive, SHELDUCK-like (p. 42), but larger, longer necked and legged than Shelduck with prominent **white wing flashes** in flight. Young lack chestnut face and neck markings and have grey legs and bill. Swims readily and dives well, especially when flightless with moult. Voice: deep quacking call and quiet whistling note.

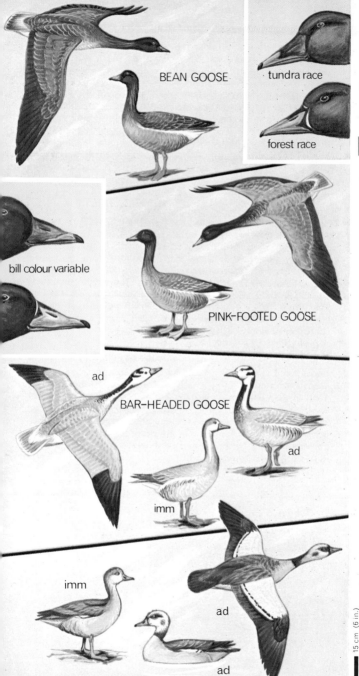

BEAN GOOSE

tundra race

forest race

bill colour variable

PINK-FOOTED GOOSE

ad

BAR-HEADED GOOSE

ad

imm

imm

ad

ad

EGYPTIAN GOOSE

15 cm (6 in.)

GEESE (ANSERIFORMES; ANATIDAE)

Brent Goose *Branta bernicla*: 55–60 cm (22–25″) Winters in coastal areas from southern Scandinavia to Biscay, and throughout England and Ireland. Occurs, often in large parties, on estuaries and mud-flats, roosting on sea at high tide and at night. **Small**, MALLARD-sized (p. 32) **goose** having a short **neck with white marks** on side and all-black head. Immatures lack white neck mark. Swims readily and will up-end to feed. Fast flight with rather rapid wing-beats, appearing to be an all-dark duck with white rear-quarters. Flocks fly low over water in extended line or compact flock of changing shape. Two races occur in region, the dark-bellied race from arctic Europe in the east, and pale-bellied race from Greenland in west, but both can occur together. Voice: croaking '*unk, unk*', producing a growling effect when birds in flock.

Barnacle Goose *Branta leucopsis*: 58–70 cm (23–27″) Winter visitor to coastal areas of southern Scandinavia, Netherlands, Germany, Scotland and Ireland. Small summering and breeding population in Sweden. Escapees from waterfowl collections not infrequent elsewhere in region, often associating with CANADA GEESE flocks. Gregarious, favouring estuaries and mud-flats, grazing at night and rarely sitting on sea. Less wary than many species of geese, flocks flying in straggling groups. Distinctly marked species with **white face pattern, black breast** and small black bill. Voice: single, repeated yapping or barking cry.

Canada Goose *Branta canadensis*: 90–105 cm (35–41″) An introduced species now resident throughout British Isles and southern Sweden. Some Swedish birds winter on German and Dutch coast. Found on wide variety of water areas, gravel pits, reservoirs, town ponds, etc., grazing on nearby grassland and crops, and nesting on suitable islands. Largest of the black geese, and the only one to be found regularly inland where frequently very tame. Heavy in appearance, with **white chin**, long dark neck and contrasting **pale breast** and brown body. Walks and swims with ease, will up-end to feed and occasionally, especially when young, dive from surface. Runs across water or land to take flight, when rather ponderous, and usually flocks take up V-formation when travelling any distance. Voice: double honking call, particularly noisy in flight or when breeding.

BRENT GOOSE

dark-bellied race

pale-bellied race

imm

ad

BARNACLE GOOSE

CANADA GOOSE

gosling

15 cm (6 in.)

SWANS (ANSERIFORMES; ANATIDAE)

Mute Swan *Cygnus olor*: 145–155 cm (57–61″) Familiar resident species found throughout British Isles and from southern Sweden westwards to central France. Some birds move further west in cold winters. Tame or partially domesticated birds, frequent almost any water area from town ponds and reservoirs to small dykes and ditches, building huge nests beside the water. Large size, white plumage and bright **orange bill with black knob** at base makes adults unmistakable. Occasional young birds have all-white plumage, but not the bright bill. Frequently rests on water with one foot outstretched beside tail and above surface. Aggressive display distinctive with wings partially raised, neck laid back and pushing itself through water with short powerful thrusts. Normally **swims with curved neck**. Walks with heavy waddling gait, but will leave water to graze or feed on crops, sometimes in large herds, but rarely more than one pair on any water when breeding, except in areas of well-known colonies. Takes flight with difficulty, running along surface of water or land to gain lift for heavy body. In flight, wings produce distinct throbbing noise, with head held stationary and neck moving up and down. When landing, feet thrust forward as brake. Voice: mainly silent, but has variety of hissing and grunting notes when aggressive.

Whooper Swan *Cygnus cygnus*: 150–155 cm (59–61″) Breeds in northern and central Scandinavia, wintering in coastal areas of North Sea, northern Britain and Ireland. Size of MUTE, but slimmer build, slightly longer **neck carried straight** when swimming and tail rarely held as high above water. Distribution of **yellow and black on bill** distinctive. Longer legged than Mute, less ungainly on land, and feet just visible beyond rather shorter tail when flying. Immatures rather greyer than Mute and lacking black at base of bill. Wings whistle in flight, less noisy than Mute. Voice: goose-like double note frequently used when flying.

Bewick's Swan *Cygnus bewickii*: 120–125 cm (47–49″) Winter visitor to southern North Sea west to Ireland. Smaller than other swans, but appearance resembles WHOOPER with shorter, rather thicker, **straight neck** and **distinctive bill pattern**. Flight more rapid, with markedly faster wing-beats than other swans. Shorter legged than Whooper and less inclined to feed on dry land, preferring shallow water areas. Winter flocks can be considerably larger than concentrations of Whoopers. Voice: double *'ooo,ooo'*, more musical and softer than Whooper.

cygnet

MUTE SWAN

ad

imm

WHOOPER SWAN

ad

imm

BEWICK'S SWAN

ad

imm

15 cm (6 in.)

EAGLES and HAWKS (FALCONIFORMES; ACCIPITRIDAE)
Flesh-eating birds of prey with strong bills and powerful talons, often with persistent soaring flight. Broad or rounded wings distinguish them from the pointed-winged falcons. Wide plumage variation makes identification difficult, structure (size and shape of wings and tail) often providing most reliable characters. Females generally larger than males, young birds sometimes taking several years to obtain adult plumage.

Golden Eagle *Aquila chrysaetos*: 75–90 cm (30–35″)   Largely resident in mountainous, almost treeless areas of Scandinavia and Scotland, usually nesting on inaccessible ledges. Often has favourite perch where will sit for long periods almost motionless. **Plumage** always appears **dark**, adult showing paler area on head and immatures with white base to tail and on wing joints. Powerful flier, with deep wing-beats and striking soaring and gliding flight often sustained for long periods when like a large BUZZARD (p. 60) with wing-tips splayed and upturned (the only eagle to soar with wings held in shallow V). Apart from size, soaring birds differ from Buzzard in having **heavy head** and **neck projecting forward**, and **long tail**. The tail is longer than in any other large eagle, being approximately equal to width of wings at base. When soaring, edges of rather long wings are not parallel, bulging slightly on trailing edge and narrowing towards outer section of fingered tips. Hunts largely by quartering mountainsides, surprising prey in open, although will take birds in flight, and regularly feeds on carrion. Voice: usually silent, but has Buzzard-like mewing call and shrill yelp or barking note.

White-tailed Eagle *Haliaeetus albicilla*: 70–90 cm (28–35″)   Breeds in coastal areas of Scandinavia, wintering southwards in extreme east of region. Largely found on rocky coasts and extensive lakes, but also occurs in wooded areas with some water. Feeds largely on fish and aquatic birds but will also scavenge along water's edge. Catches fish by plunging feet first into water. When perched, legs not fully feathered, and closed wing-tips just reach to end of tail (wings markedly shorter than tail in GOLDEN EAGLE). Less inclined to soar than Golden Eagle, but massive build distinctive with very broad, square-ended wings with parallel edges held flat (not in V). Head and neck protrude well beyond wings, making heavy bill obvious, while **short wedge-shaped tail** (white in adult, dark in immature) projects as far behind as head in front. Flight rather heavy, recalling vulture, often flapping with relatively shallow wing-beats low over water or vegetation.   Voice: deep barking note.

GOLDEN EAGLE

ad

imm

imm

ad

imm

WHITE-TAILED EAGLE

15 cm (6 in.)

EAGLES (FALCONIFORMES; ACCIPITRIDAE)

Spotted Eagle *Aquila clanga*: 65–75 cm (26–30″) Occurs in southern Sweden as passage migrant from eastern Europe. Frequents low-lying woodland areas, but equally at home in open country when on passage, when feeds mainly on slow-moving ground animals, reptiles, etc. Confusion is most likely with LESSER SPOTTED EAGLE although immatures bear some resemblance to WHITE-TAILED EAGLE (p. 56). **Immature has** distinct whitish area at base of tail, conspicuous **large pale spots on upper-parts** (larger and covering greater area than immature Lesser Spotted) and pale area on under-side at joint of wing (less distinct in immature Lesser Spotted). Adults have greatly reduced pale area at base of tail (still obvious in adult Lesser Spotted) and appear all dark. Soars less frequently than other eagles, but when soaring and gliding the broad, square-cut wings (broader than Lesser Spotted) are held with leading edge straight and slightly drooping, giving a rather heron-like (p. 26) appearance when viewed head on. Small head and bill (smaller headed than Lesser Spotted) on short neck does not project far beyond wings, while short, slightly wedge-shaped tail gives effect of short-necked White-tailed. Tail length about half width of wing, with broader tail base than Lesser Spotted. Flight is heavy and laboured, giving clumsy appearance, but wing-beats deeper than Lesser Spotted. Voice: resembles barking of small dog.

Lesser Spotted Eagle *Aquila pomarina*: 60–65 cm (24–26″) Summer visitor to forest areas of north Germany, but hunting in more open country where it quarters the ground for small mammals. When settled on ground can walk with ease. Slightly smaller than, but easily confused with, SPOTTED EAGLE (see that species for distinguishing characters). White at base of tail and at joint on upper-surface of wings present at all ages. White spots on wings of immature form two distinct lines, but only one visible in flight. Wings held flat when soaring, slightly drooping when gliding, and slightly forward of right-angles with body. Wings narrower than Spotted, with edges almost parallel. **Tail rounded** not wedge shaped, and longer than Spotted. Flight less heavy than Spotted with shallower wing-beats. Voice: similar to Spotted, but much shriller.

SPOTTED EAGLE

ad

imm

ad

imm

ad

imm

LESSER SPOTTED EAGLE

ad

imm

15 cm (6 in.)

BUZZARDS (FALCONIFORMES; ACCIPITRIDAE)

Buzzard *Buteo buteo*: 50–55 cm (20–22″) Summer visitor to central-northern Scandinavia, resident from southern Scandinavia westwards except Ireland where absent, and south-east England where scarce. Nests mainly in trees, inhabiting woodland or areas of scattered trees, wintering in more open hilly or moorland country. Hunts principally for rabbits, but regularly feeds on carrion. Commonest of the buzzards, with extremely variable plumage. Spends a considerable time soaring on broad rounded wings and tail, with wings held raised above horizontal and wing-tip feathers widely spread and further up-curved. Widely fanned tail has length equal to three-quarters width of wing base. Head, on short thick neck, does not project far beyond wings. **Tail barred** with narrow indistinct bars for its entire length, with broader bar at tip. Flight usually slow and ponderous with wing-flaps less deep than HONEY BUZZARD. Voice: high-pitched, gull-like mewing.

Rough-legged Buzzard *Buteo lagopus*: 50–60 cm (20–24″) Breeds in northern Scandinavia, wintering south from southern Scandinavia to eastern Britain, but numbers vary greatly from year to year. Found in open or mountainous country, nesting on cliff ledges. Hunts for a variety of mammals, frequently hovering with slow heavy wing-beats. The most distinctive of the buzzards, with less plumage variation than other species. Characteristically has **wide black band at tip of pale tail**, dark marks at joints on under-side of pale wings, and dark belly patch contrasting with pale head. Tail and wings longer and narrower than BUZZARD, tail length about equal width of wings at base. Head broad, on short neck, and not projecting far beyond wings. When perched, feathered legs distinguish from other buzzards. Flight is less stiff winged than other buzzards. Voice: louder, higher pitched than Buzzard.

Honey Buzzard *Pernis apivorus*: 50–60 cm (20–24″) Summer visitor to region, north to central Sweden and southern England. Tree-nesting in deciduous woodland areas. Feeds mainly on insects, robbing bees' and wasps' nests, and spends more time on ground than other buzzards. Confusion likely with BUZZARD and, as with that species, has a wide variety of plumage. Most characteristic features are **two broad** dark **bars at base of tail** and third at tip, and barring on under-side of flight feathers, but these features are not easily seen. Slimmer bodied than Buzzard, with smaller head on longer neck, protruding well beyond wings to give a rather pigeon-like effect. Wings longer, tail narrower, with square end and slightly longer than width of wings at base. Spends less time in air than Buzzard, soaring with wings held flat, but slightly drooped when gliding. Flight has very deep wing-beats. Voice: double '*pee-ah*'.

plumage variable

BUZZARD

ROUGH-LEGGED
BUZZARD

HONEY BUZZARD

plumage variable

15 cm (6 in.)

HAWKS (FALCONIFORMES; ACCIPITRIDAE)

Sparrowhawk *Accipiter nisus*: Male 25–33 cm (10–13"); female 30–38 cm (12–15") Resident throughout region except northern Scandinavia where summer visitor only. Inhabits woodland areas, nesting for preference in conifers. Feeds on small birds which are caught by rapid dashes through trees or along hedgerows and taken to regularly used feeding posts. Flight usually close to ground, but will soar, usually in circles with occasional series of wing-beats. Distinguished from other birds of prey by **short**, broad, **rounded wings** and **long tail**. Similarly shaped but larger GOSHAWK has relatively shorter tail. Flying birds can resemble CUCKOO (p. 142). Marked size difference between sexes; the larger female is darker and browner than grey male, and males appear to have less rounded wings in flight. Very brown immatures are streaked, not barred, on under-parts. Voice: chattering *'kew, kew, kew'* in rapid series of several notes.

Goshawk *Accipiter gentilis*: Male 48–55 cm (19–22"); female 53–60 cm (21–24") Resident throughout region except northernmost Scandinavia where summer visitor and British Isles where occasional visitor to south. Inhabits forest areas but much scarcer than similarly built but smaller SPARROW-HAWK, with proportionately shorter tail. Flight and behaviour resemble Sparrowhawk. Plumage dark, contrasting with **pale stripe over eye** and **very white** and prominent **under-tail coverts**. Female much larger than male; immatures streaked, adults barred. Voice: shrill, screaming *'ka-ka-ka'* in rapid series of notes.

Red Kite *Milvus milvus*: 60 cm (24") Resident in central Wales, otherwise summer visitor to region north to central France and southern Scandinavia. Inhabits areas of deciduous woodland and scattered trees, feeding largely on carrion. Slim bodied, with long, angled wings and long, **deeply forked tail**, showing some indentation even when fully spread. Rather dark **rufous plumage** contrasts with pale head and striking white wing-patches. Soars with angled wings, slightly arched, and constantly moving tail. Flight graceful, with body moving up and down with wing-beats. For differences from BLACK KITE see that species.

Black Kite *Milvus migrans*: 55 cm (22") Summer visitor to region except British Isles, northern France and Scandinavia. Inhabits variety of areas, often near human habitation or water, feeding by scavenging. Could be confused with MARSH HARRIER (p. 64) but **glides with wings level** or arched and frequent twists of tail. Thicker set than RED KITE with **tail** shorter, less forked and appearing **square-ended** when fully spread, and lacking reddish coloration when viewed against light. Generally lacks plumage contrast of Red Kite, appearing more uniform and darker. More communal than Red Kite, often in large parties at food source.

62

SPARROWHAWK

♂ ad

♀ imm

♂ imm

♀ ad

ad ♂

GOSHAWK

imm ♀

♂ imm

imm

RED KITE

ad

imm

BLACK KITE

ad

15 cm (6 in.)

HARRIERS (FALCONIFORMES; ACCIPITRIDAE)

Marsh Harrier *Circus aeruginosus*: 48–55 cm (19–22") Summer visitor to southern Scandinavia and east of region; resident in west, north to south-east England. Inhabits marshes and large reed-beds, wintering in many coastal areas. Hunts by quartering low over ground, dropping on to prey, predominantly mammals and birds. Most distinctive of the harriers, but retaining the generally slim-bodied, narrow-winged, long-tailed and small-headed appearance of these birds. **Broad bodied**, with broader, more **rounded wings** than other harriers, females lacking white rump and males without the over-all pale grey plumage. Immatures resemble females. Larger than other harriers, with less graceful, more BUZZARD-like (p. 60) flight. When gliding or soaring can be confused with Buzzard or BLACK KITE (p. 62), but differs from former by being much longer tailed, and from latter by wings held in deep V and tail-end rounded. Voice: generally silent, but variety of shrill cries and alarm notes on breeding ground.

Hen Harrier *Circus cyaneus*: 40–50 cm (16–20") Found throughout region in suitable areas of moorland or open country. In winter, inhabits wetter, more marshland sites. Hunts in typical harrier fashion. Narrower winged and less bulky than MARSH HARRIER, appearing shorter winged than other harriers. Wings held raised when soaring or gliding, and in flight wing-beats faster than Marsh Harrier. Plumage closely resembles MONTAGU'S HARRIER. Males have grey upper-parts with prominent black primaries and **white rump**; under-parts white with black primaries and dark trailing edge to under-wing. Females have dark brown upper-parts with prominent white rump; under-parts streaked, with bars on wings and tail. Immatures indistinguishable from females. Voice: chattering Sparrowhawk-like (p. 62) cry on breeding grounds.

Montagu's Harrier *Circus pygargus*: 40–45 cm (16–18") Summer visitor to south of region, as far north as southern England and Sweden. Favours marshes and young plantations where behaviour resembles other harriers. Slimmer bodied, narrower winged and more buoyant flight than other harriers. Most closely resembles HEN HARRIER. Males have darker grey upper-parts with no white rump and small **black bar on upper-wing**; under-parts less white with black primaries and some dark barring on under-wing. Females very similar to Hen Harrier, at times indistinguishable, but body slimmer, wings narrower and appearing longer. White rump usually smaller and under-parts less well barred, secondaries often appearing as a complete dark area. Head of female shows distinctive dark mark on side of face. Immatures resemble females but have unstreaked, rich chestnut-buff under-parts. Voice: typical chattering call on breeding grounds is quieter than Hen Harrier.

MARSH HARRIER

♂

♂

♀ & imm

♀ & imm

♂

HEN HARRIER

♂

♀ & imm

♀ & imm

♂

♀

imm

imm

MONTAGU'S HARRIER

15 cm (6 in.)

EAGLES (FALCONIFORMES; ACCIPITRIDAE)

Booted Eagle *Hieraeetus pennatus*: 45–55 cm (18–22″) Summer visitor to central France, inhabiting wooded hill country and nesting in tall trees. BUZZARD-sized (p. 60) eagle with buzzard-like shape but longer tail, and wings more angled when gliding. **Flight buoyant** and fast, with **deep wing-beats** and regular periods of gliding. Soars with wings held level. Occurs in two distinct colour phases, the more numerous pale phase with strongly **contrasting under-wing pattern** is distinctive and unlikely to be confused with other birds of prey. Less common dark phase with generally uniform plumage and slightly paler tail can look similar to MARSH HARRIER (p. 64) or BLACK KITE (p. 62), but wings always broader, and flight distinct, harrier carrying wings in unmistakable V when soaring. Tail of kite looks slightly forked or square when spread; eagle has rounded tail when spread. Voice: shrill double note.

Short-toed Eagle *Circaetus gallicus*: 65–70 cm (26–28″) Summer visitor to southern France, inhabiting open country with some woodland and nesting on the tops of trees. Rather **small, pale** eagle, only slightly larger than BUZZARD (p. 60), but with long, broad, square-ended wings and tail equal to or a little shorter than breadth of wings at base. Rather broad, rounded head can appear owl-like. Flight strong, purposeful, with deep wing-beats; but soars with wings held flat. Hovers regularly when hunting; only bird of prey to feed predominantly on snakes, and individuals may be seen carrying snakes in flight. Extent of **dark markings on under-parts** vary, but majority have only breast, throat, wing-tips and bars on tail dark. Voice: Buzzard-like mewing cry.

OSPREYS (FALCONIFORMES; PANDIONIDAE)

Osprey *Pandion haliaetus*: 50–60 cm (20–24″) Summer visitor to Scandinavia, north Germany and highlands of Scotland; tree-nesting in woodland or moorland areas associated with water. Migrants occur throughout region, but scarce in Ireland. Distinctive bird of prey, with contrasting **black-and-white plumage** and rather gull-like appearance. Flies rather slowly with loose flapping flight and frequent glides. Hunts by diving for fish from air, entering water feet first; hunting sometimes accompanied by ponderous hovering. **Flies with angled wings**, and soars with wings bowed, easily confused with large gull at a distance, but black-and-white patterning on under-parts distinctive. Frequently perches on exposed sites overlooking water, and carries fish in talons to regularly used feeding perches. Voice: shrill piping note.

BOOTED EAGLE

pale phase   dark phase

SHORT-TOED EAGLE

markings vary

OSPREY

15 cm (6 in.)

FALCONS (FALCONIFORMES; FALCONIDAE) *Birds of prey with rapid wing-beats and fast flight. Shape distinctive, with long tails and pointed wings. Most species have strong moustachial stripes; sexes similar, but females usually larger than males. Most species feed by diving rapidly at prey.*

Hobby *Falco subbuteo*: 30–55 cm (12–14″) Summer visitor to western Europe, but absent from northern Scandinavia, northern Britain and Ireland; inhabiting scattered woodland and nesting in trees. Very active falcon, resembling **small** PEREGRINE with comparatively shorter tail and **swift-like** (p. 144) **silhouette**. Very manoeuvrable flight, hunting on wing for large flying insects, feeding in flight by passing prey to bill. Often to be found hunting amongst swallow and martin flocks. Voice: distinct repeated *'cew'* or rapid chattering *'kekekekeke'*.

Peregrine *Falco peregrinus*: 38–51 cm (15–20″) Resident throughout north-west Europe apart from northernmost Scandinavia, where summer visitor only, and lowland areas in England and around southern North Sea where winter visitor only. Inhabits rocky or mountainous country, nesting on both inland and coastal cliffs. Found in more low-lying, marshland areas in winter. **Large falcon** with **heavy moustachial streak** and fast, powerful, active flight interspersed with frequent glides somewhat similar to a pigeon. Will soar, often diving strongly from height at tremendous speed with wings almost closed. Feeds mainly on birds, often as large as ducks or pigeons, which are taken in flight and carried to regularly used plucking posts. Will sit motionless on exposed perch for long periods. Voice: very variable, typical call a chattering *'kec-kec-kec'*.

Gyrfalcon *Falco rusticolus*: 50–55 cm (20–22″) Confined to Scandinavia, where inhabits coastal cliffs and mountainous areas. **Largest** European **falcon**, resembling a large, heavy-bodied PEREGRINE with slower wing-beats and over-all **pale plumage** lacking strong moustachial stripes. Broader winged and longer tailed than Peregrine; when perched, wing-tips do not reach end of tail. Hunts low, catching prey on ground, rarely soars. Occurs in two colour phases, but many intermediates are found. Voice: usually silent, some chattering calls on breeding grounds.

Saker Falcon *Falco cherrug*: 45–50 cm (18–20″) Summer visitor to southern Germany, inhabiting open country with scattered woodland. Powerful falcon, appearing broader winged and longer tailed than similar-sized PEREGRINE. **Pale head** contrasting with **brown back**, and lack of strong moustachial stripes are distinctive features. Voice: shrill *'ki-ki-ki'* call.

HOBBY

ad   imm

ad   imm

PEREGRINE

ad

imm

ad   imm

GYRFALCON

pale phase

imm

dark phase

plumage
extremely
variable

ad   imm

SAKER FALCON

ad   imm

15 cm (6 in.)

FALCONS (FALCONIFORMES; FALCONIDAE)

Merlin *Falco columbarius*: 28–33 cm (11–13″) Summer visitor to Scandinavia, and resident throughout much of Britain, inhabiting moorland and open country, nesting on ground or isolated trees and cliffs. Winters throughout western Europe except Scandinavia, favouring low-lying coastal areas or open country. **Smallest** European **falcon**, rather nondescript and **lacking strong plumage markings**. Shorter tailed than KESTREL, with compact shape, wings kept closer to body in flight. Dashing flight action is usually low and interspersed with short glides. Hunts by chasing small birds, following twists and turns of prey; using favoured perches such as prominent rocks or fences as plucking places. Voice: shrill, chattering '*kik-kik-kik*', similar to other falcons.

Red-footed Falcon *Falco vespertinus*: 28–30 cm (11–12″) Passage migrant to south-east of region from breeding grounds in eastern Europe, favouring open country with scattered woodland. HOBBY-shaped (p. 68) falcon with longer wings, broader at the base. Wing-tips reach end of tail when perched. **All-dark male** distinctive, **females and immatures** somewhat similar to Hobby, but **have pale heads** and less marked under-parts. Frequently occurs in flocks or small groups. Glides and hovers when hunting, most frequently taken prey being large flying insects which are eaten in flight. Will hunt by dropping from perch on to ground prey. Particularly active at dusk. Hovering is less persistent than that of KESTREL and body is usually held in more upright position, but this varies with strength of wind. Voice: typical falcon chattering, but very high pitched.

Kestrel *Falco tinnunculus*: 33–36 cm (13–14″) Resident throughout north-west Europe, except northern Scandinavia where summer visitor only. Found in wide variety of habitats from cliffs and moorland to farmland and town centres. Nests on trees, buildings or ledges. The commonest and most familiar of the falcons, with distinctive **hovering flight** used for hunting ground-living prey. In towns, feeds largely on sparrows which are caught by chasing. Usually solitary, long pointed wings and very long tail giving distinctive outline. Flies with rapid wing-beats and short glides. Hovers with tail fanned, periods of hovering interspersed with short glides as moves to new position, or rapid decrease in height before hovering closer to ground. Voice: loud, shrill '*kee-kee-kee*'.

MERLIN

♀

♂

♂

♀

imm

RED-FOOTED
FALCON

hovering

KESTREL

♂

♀

15 cm (6 in.)

GROUSE (GALLIFORMES; TETRAONIDAE) *Stocky ground-living game birds of open country. Short winged, with heavy, direct, whirring flight. Nostrils, legs and feet covered with feathers, most species with red wattles above eyes. Ground nesting. Sexes differ, immatures resembling females. Some species with distinctive winter plumage.*

Red Grouse *Lagopus lagopus*: 37–42 cm (14–17") Resident in Scandinavia, northern and western Britain, inhabiting open areas of scrub, moorland and tundra. Will occur on farmland in winter. Occurs in two distinct races, birds from the British Isles remaining all dark throughout year; birds from Scandinavia (Willow Grouse) have wings and belly white in summer, becoming all white except for dark tail in winter. Birds from coastal areas of Norway tend to be intermediate between these. Most likely confusion is with PTARMIGAN, but less grey with stouter bill and no black face patch, and inhabiting lower altitudes. Lack of white in plumage of British birds distinguishes from much larger male BLACK GROUSE, while female Black Grouse lacks contrasting wings and tail. Flight is rapid, close to ground, periods of wing-beats interspersed with glides on down-curved wings. Often flocks into parties of one sex during winter. Voice: loud, far-carrying '*coc-oc-oc*' and call likened to 'go-back, go-back'.

Ptarmigan *Lagopus mutus*: 36 cm (14") Resident in Scotland, northern and western Scandinavia, inhabiting mountainous country above tree-line; invariably at higher altitude than RED GROUSE. Resembles Scandinavian Red Grouse in winter, but smaller bill and males have black patch between bill and eye, and black tail is tipped white. Generally yellower than Red Grouse in summer, becoming greyer in autumn plumage. Often tame and approachable, appearing reluctant to fly, but closely resembles grouse in flight, although flies up vertical mountain slopes with ease. Flocks in winter and non-breeding males often form summer parties. Voice: hoarse, crackling, cough-like note.

Black Grouse *Lyrurus tetrix*: Male 50–53 cm (20–21"); female 41–43 cm (16–17") Resident from eastern France and Germany north throughout Scandinavia; also in Wales, northern England and Scotland. Inhabits moors and heaths and areas of scattered woodland. Often found in large numbers at communal display grounds. Males distinctive, **females** differ from RED GROUSE by greyer plumage, **forked tail** and narrow **pale wing-bars**. Voice: displaying male has wide variety of crowing calls, otherwise a double sneezing note.

RED GROUSE

♂ Scand. summer

♀ British race ♂

♀ Scand. summer

♂ Scand. intermediate

♂ Scand. winter

♂ winter

♀ summer ♂

♀ winter

♂ autumn

winter ♀

PTARMIGAN

BLACK GROUSE

♂

♀

males displaying

♂

15 cm (6 in.)

GROUSE (GALLIFORMES; TETRAONIDAE)

Capercaillie *Tetrao urogallus*: Male 84–86 cm (33–34″); female 58–62 cm (23–24″) Resident in Scandinavia, Scotland and southern Germany, inhabiting coniferous forests in mountainous and upland country; will move to more lowland woods in winter. Virtually unmistakable, **largest grouse** of the region, with conspicuous long, broad, **fan-shaped tail**. Female much larger than female BLACK GROUSE (p. 72) and differs by rufous colour of breast and lack of forked tail. Feathers of neck and throat can be raised to produce whiskered effect. Rather shy and secretive. Mainly found on ground, but perches readily in trees, particularly in winter; takes flight from branches with much noise as flies through outer foliage. Flight rapid and direct, periods of wing-beats interspersed with glides on down-curved wings. During display male raises and fans tail, stretches neck and points head upwards. Voice: wide variety of calls on communal display ground, variously likened to drawing of cork, pouring water out of bottle, clearing throat and loud rattle.

Hazelhen *Tetrastes bonasia*: 35–36 cm (14″) Resident in south and east Scandinavia and southern Germany, inhabiting mixed woodland, usually with thick ground cover and often near water. **Smallest** of the **grouse**, and more of a woodland species, readily perching in trees. Longish tail and slight crest give a distinctive outline. Less inclined to run or crouch than other grouse, flying more readily when disturbed with wings making distinct buzzing sound and **black band** at **end of tail** striking. Rarely flies any great distance before settling. Voice: high-pitched whistle.

PHEASANTS and PARTRIDGES (GALLIFORMES; PHASIANIDAE) *Smaller game-birds than grouse, with unfeathered legs and feet. Short rounded wings with whirring flight; pheasants with long tails, partridges (and quails) smaller and short tailed. Flocks form outside breeding season. Sexes differ in pheasants, but similar in partridges; immatures resemble female or poorly marked adult. Summer and winter plumages similar.*

Pheasant *Phasianus colchicus*: Male 65–90 cm (26–35″); female 55–65 cm (22–26″) Absent from Norway and northern Sweden, elsewhere resident, inhabiting scattered woods, thickets, hedgerows, farmland, etc. Commonest, most widespread and familiar game bird of region with distinctive **long tail**. When disturbed will usually run, but will burst into flight, often exploding from cover. An introduced species into western Europe and populations vary greatly in appearance, the result of the introduction of numerous different races from Asia. Most varying features of males' plumage are darkness and redness of body feathers and presence or absence of white neck-ring. Voice: various cackling and chuckling notes, male has loud harsh crowing and double bark.

CAPERCAILLIE

♀

displaying ♂

♀ HAZELHEN

♂

♂

♀

PHEASANT

♀

♂

plumage extremely variable   ♂ Pheasants

15 cm (6 in.)

PHEASANTS and PARTRIDGES (GALLIFORMES; PHASIA-NIDAE)

Red-legged Partridge *Alectoris rufa*: 35 cm (14″)   Resident in western France, eastern and southern England; inhabiting a wide variety of open country, including farmland and waste ground. Prefers drier and stonier areas than PARTRIDGE. Larger, heavier bodied than Partridge with strong **contrasting head and flank patterns**. Juveniles lack striking coloration of adults, but parties of juveniles tend to be accompanied by adults. Flocks, or coveys, form outside breeding season, but these often scatter when disturbed. Less inclined to fly than Partridge, disturbed birds preferring to run. Movements on ground are quicker and more jerking than Partridge. Voice: harsh double call, *'chucka chucka'*.

Partridge *Perdix perdix*: 30 cm (12″)   Resident throughout region, except northernmost Scandinavia, where absent. In-habits all types of open country, favouring arable farmland and downs. Commonest and most widespread partridge of western Europe. Lacks contrasting plumage of RED-LEGGED PARTRIDGE, juveniles somewhat resembling young PHEASANTS (p. 74), but are more streaked with short tail. Family parties of young birds can be confused with QUAIL but generally lack head markings. Exclusively ground living, taking flight with whirring wings and flying strongly, usually close to ground and rarely for any distance. Walks with distinct **round-backed appearance**, although if alarmed stretches neck and runs rapidly. Will crouch motionless. Families remain together in covey throughout winter. Voice: grating *'kirr-it, kirr-it'* likened to rusty door-hinge or turning key.

Quail *Coturnix coturnix*: 18 cm (7″)   Summer visitor to region, arriving during May and early June, north to Scotland and southern Scandinavia, but northern limit and numbers vary greatly from year to year. Predominantly a bird of grassland and growing crops. **Smallest European game bird** and only species to occur in region exclusively as summer visitor. Differs from young PARTRIDGE by streaked head pattern, lack of chestnut on tail, and black throat markings of male. Similar-sized CORNCRAKE (p. 80) flies with dangling legs and has prominent chestnut wing flashes. Habits and actions resemble Partridge, forming parties or bevies after breeding and on migration. Flight action with typical whirring of game birds, but secretive and difficult to see, usually only **flushed underfoot**. Usually heard rather than seen. Voice: distinctive trisyllabic call, usually rendered as *'wet-my-lips'* with a very liquid quality.

RED-LEGGED PARTRIDGE

imm

ad

PARTRIDGE

ad

imm

QUAIL

imm

ad

15 cm (6 in.)

PHEASANTS and PARTRIDGES (GALLIFORMES; PHASIANIDAE)

FERAL GAME BIRDS Over a number of years, attempts have been made to introduce many species of Asian and American game birds into western Europe for sporting purposes. Many of these attempts have been unsuccessful or are in need of continual releases to maintain the numbers. A few species have apparently established self-supporting feral populations living in the wild; and although the majority are still very restricted in distribution, the following seven species could be encountered in a fully wild condition by European bird-watchers.

Golden Pheasant *Chrysolophus pictus*: Male 120 cm (47″) but 68 cm (28″) of tail; female 61 cm (24″) but 35 cm (14″) of tail. Asiatic woodland species established in England and Scotland.

Lady Amherst's Pheasant *Chrysolophus amherstiae*: Male 127 cm (50″) but 91 cm (36″) of tail; female 61 cm (24″) but 35 cm (14″) of tail. Asiatic woodland species established in England. Female closely resembles female GOLDEN PHEASANT but differs in having blue-grey legs and bare skin, and lacks red around eye.

Silver Pheasant *Lophura nycthemera*: Male 120 cm (47″) but 60 cm (24″) of tail; female 52 cm (20″) but 25 cm (10″) of tail. Asiatic woodland species established in Germany.

Reeve's Pheasant *Syrmaticus reevesii*: Male 198 cm (78″) but 150 cm (59″) of tail; female 80 cm (32″) but 42 cm (17″) of tail. Asiatic woodland species established in Scotland, France and Germany.

Bobwhite *Colinus virginianus*: 22 cm (9″) American open scrubland and farmland species established in England and Germany.

California Quail *Lophortyx californicus*: 25 cm (10″) American open scrubland species established in Germany.

TURKEYS (GALLIFORMES; MELEAGRIDIDAE)

Wild Turkey *Meleagris gallopavo*: 102–110 cm (40–43″) American woodland species established in Germany.

GOLDEN PHEASANT

♀

♂

LADY
AMHERST'S
PHEASANT

♂

SILVER
PHEASANT

♂

♀

♀

REEVE'S
PHEASANT

♂

WILD
TURKEY

Scale for this section
BOBWHITE

♀

♂

♀

♂

CALIFORNIA
QUAIL

15 cm (6 in.)

CRAKES (GRUIFORMES; RALLIDAE) *Shy, ground-living birds inhabiting wet areas. More frequently heard than seen, skulking, rarely fly, when short, rounded wings and dangling legs distinctive. Sexes similar.*

Spotted Crake *Porzana porzana*: 23 cm (9″) Resident in western France and small numbers in southern England, otherwise summer visitor north to central Scandinavia. Inhabits ponds, marshes and ditches with dense vegetation, most active at dusk when will feed in open. Usually solitary, moving with frequent upward jerks of tail, especially when alarmed. Somewhat resembles short-billed WATER RAIL (p. 82), but prominent **white spots on upper-parts** and **buff under tail** coverts are distinctive. Voice: rhythmic ticking note and high-pitched, repeated call said to resemble cracking of whip.

Baillon's Crake *Porzana pusilla*: 18 cm (7″) Summer visitor to western France and a few isolated sites in south of region. Extremely skulking in dense vegetation of swamps and ponds. Small size and difficulty of observing makes the species hard to separate from male LITTLE CRAKE. Both sexes have rufous upper-parts with prominent white streaks on wing coverts, and **flanks boldly barred black and white.** The all-green bill lacks red bands of Little Crake, and legs are flesh-pink. Immatures closely resemble immature Little Crake but have stronger barring on flanks. Voice: apparently resembles Little Crake and confusion can result in separating the two. Trilling call usually heard at dusk or night is said to be faster and higher pitched than that of Little Crake and is often introduced by a few slower notes.

Little Crake *Porzana parva*: 19 cm (7·5″) Summer visitor to extreme south-east of region. Inhabits similar areas to other crakes but has preference for high reed-beds or water sites with floating mats of vegetation. Male differs from similar BAILLON'S by having olive-brown, not rufous upper-parts, lacking white streaks on wing coverts and no strong black-and-white barring on flanks, although remainder of under-parts are as Baillon's Crake. Female resembles immature of the two species, but with red base to yellow-green bill and bright green legs. Voice: resembles Baillon's Crake but slower and rather weaker, usually ending in rapid trill.

Corncrake *Crex crex*: 27 cm (11″) Summer visitor to region, north to central Scandinavia, although absent as a breeding bird from much of England. The only dry-habitat crake of the region, found in lush grass and crops. Very skulking, solitary and crepuscular, separated from other crakes by larger size. When viewed on ground appears very buff and short necked; while in flight, **prominent chestnut wing-patches** are distinctive, separating bird from QUAIL and young PARTRIDGE (p. 76). Voice: during breeding season distinctive, persistent call which can continue throughout night. Double rasping note, written as '*kwex, kwex*' and said to resemble grated comb.

SPOTTED CRAKE

imm

imm

BAILLON'S CRAKE

LITTLE CRAKE

♂

♀

CORNCRAKE

15 cm (6 in.)

CRAKES (GRUIFORMES; RALLIDAE)

Water Rail *Rallus aquaticus*: 28 cm (11″)   Resident through-out region except northernmost Scandinavia. Inhabits wide variety of wet-area habitats from large ponds to small dykes and ditches with dense vegetation. Difficult to observe since nervous and skulking, but only crake of region with **long bill**. Olive-brown upper-parts marked with black, strongly barred black-and-white flanks and prominent white under tail coverts very noticeable as bird disappears into cover. During cold weather, when water areas frozen, frequently feeds in open, when can be very aggressive, even attacking smaller birds. More often heard than seen. Voice: wide variety of notes often said to resemble dying pig and consisting of range of squeals, grunts and various cluckings. A sharply repeated single note can often be confused with other crakes. Very vocal at night.

Moorhen *Gallinula chloropus*: 33 cm (13″)   Resident through-out region, north to southern Scandinavia, summer visitor to central Scandinavia. Inhabits almost all freshwater sites from town ponds and lakes to small dykes and ditches margined with vegetation. Frequently leaves water to feed on surround-ing grassland. Swims readily with jerking motion of head and occasionally dives, especially when disturbed, and will remain submerged with bill just visible above water. Takes flight readily, but weak and laboured with considerable pattering along surface for take-off. Often communal in winter months, especially during cold weather, when frequent-ly found some distance from water. Readily distinguished water bird with **red forehead and base to bill**, white line along side, and white under tail which is jerked regularly when walking and swimming. More uniformly coloured brown immatures are distinguished from other water birds by white under tail. Voice: harsh, penetrating double note *'cittic'*.

Coot *Fulica atra*: 38 cm (15″)   Resident throughout region except northernmost Scandinavia. Inhabits more open water than other crakes, usually where there is some surrounding vegetation. Frequently becomes tame on town ponds and lakes. Very gregarious outside breeding season when some-times occurs on salt water, but often quarrelsome with frequent fights and chases. Only crake to habitually dive for food. Easily recognizable **all-black water bird** with white bill and forehead. In flight shows white trailing edge to wing. Browner immature has white under-parts, particularly on chin and throat, while downy chicks have very red heads. Voice: very loud and distinctive high-pitched single note *'tewk'* and variety of similar disyllabic calls.

WATER RAIL

MOORHEN

COOT

imm

imm

15 cm (6 in.)

CRANES (GRUIFORMES; GRUIDAE)

Crane *Grus grus*: 114 cm (45") Summer visitor to Scandinavia, migrating southwards through remainder of region. Inhabits large areas of marshes and wet heath avoiding wooded areas. Unmistakable, **large, long-legged, long-necked** ground-living bird, somewhat resembling stork, but basic **plumage grey** with distinctive head and neck markings. Flight on broad long wings is slow and powerful with neck extended and legs trailing behind, flocks frequently taking up V-formation. Walks with slow and graceful gait but usually shy, not allowing close approach. Immatures are browner, lacking characteristic head markings and long feathers drooping over tail. Confusion is only likely with exotic cranes which have escaped from wildfowl collections. Voice: distinctive trumpeting call and various grating and hissing notes.

BUSTARDS (GRUIFORMES; OTIDIDAE) *Large, long-necked, long-legged land birds with heavy bills, inhabiting open country; strong flight and broad wings, with neck and legs extended. Normally walk but will crouch and run when alarmed. Sexes differ, immatures resembling females.*

Great Bustard *Otis tarda*: Male 102 cm (40"); female 76 cm (30") Small numbers resident in northern Germany, inhabiting areas of extensive cereal farming. The heaviest land bird of the region, although rather shy and unapproachable. Flight powerful but with slow wing-beats and often in small flocks. Easily distinguished by large size, thick neck and legs. Both sexes show considerable amount of white in flight. Voice: low grunting note but generally rather silent.

Little Bustard *Otis tetrax*: 43 cm (17") Summer visitor to southern France, inhabiting grassy open areas or cultivated land. Extremely shy. Small size suggests a rather long-legged grouse but walk and flight typical of bustard. More mobile than GREAT BUSTARD with more rapid whistling wing-beats. Gregarious after breeding season when flying birds show tremendous extent of white on wings. Takes flight more readily than Great Bustard, less inclined to crouch and run. Voice: short coughing note in flight, and during display a far-carrying snorting call.

CRANE

imm

ad

GREAT BUSTARD

♂

♀

♂

LITTLE BUSTARD

♀

15 cm (6 in.)

OYSTERCATCHERS (CHARADRIIFORMES; HAEMATOPODIDAE)

Oystercatcher *Haematopus ostralegus*: 43 cm (17″)   Resident in coastal areas throughout region, except Scandinavia where summer visitor only in north. Distinctive black-and-white shore wader with **long red bill** and pink legs. White throat of winter plumage sometimes retained throughout summer by non-breeding birds. Very noisy; outside breeding season sometimes in large flocks feeding on sandy or muddy shores and resting on fields or islands between tides. Flight strong but wing-beat shallow, when prominent white wing-bar apparent. Voice: series of shrill, strident and penetrating calls are used in the breeding season and during winter months.

PLOVERS (CHARADRIIFORMES; CHARADRIIDAE) *Short-billed, generally short-necked wading birds with compact form and distinctive feeding action, running forward for short distances then tilting body forward to pick food from surface. Frequently 'bob' body when alarmed. Many species with distinctive head and neck markings. Sexes similar. Winter plumage usually less well marked. Immatures resemble adults in winter.*

Lapwing *Vanellus vanellus*: 30 cm (12″)   Resident throughout region except Scandinavia where summer visitor only in north. Familiar bird of farm and grassland, moving to wetter areas, frequently on coast, during winter months. Highly gregarious, and very distinctive, with general **black-and-white appearance** and **broad, rounded wings**. During breeding season has highly characteristic display flight, when wings make loud throbbing noise and bird tumbles in sky. Voice: highly vocal at all times, particularly during display, typical call being *'pee-wit'* or variation on this theme.

Turnstone *Arenaria interpres*: 23 cm (9″)   Summer visitor to coastal areas of Scandinavia, found in winter in coastal areas throughout remainder of region. Inhabits rocky weed-covered shore, often mixing with PURPLE SANDPIPER (p. 104). Appears basically black and white both at rest and in flight, contrasting with bright orange legs. Feeds by turning over stones and seaweed. Voice: one or more rather slurred twittering notes and a harder grunting disyllabic call.

OYSTERCATCHER

winter

LAPWING

ad

imm

TURNSTONE

summer

winter

15 cm (6 in.)

PLOVERS (CHARADRIIFORMES; CHARADRIIDAE)

Ringed Plover *Charadrius hiaticula*: 19 cm (7·5″) Summer visitor to Scandinavia and coastal areas of southern North Sea, resident in British Isles and winter visitor to coastal France. Inhabits sandy or stony beaches, moving to more muddy coastal sites in winter, rarely found inland. One of the commonest shore birds with very active behaviour. Generally plump with distinctive **black-and-white head and breast markings**. Differs from similar LITTLE RINGED PLOVER by having larger, heavier head, lack of eye-ring, brighter legs and prominent white wing-bar in flight. Flight rapid, with regular wing-beats but during display a distinctive wavering, side-to-side flight takes place over breeding territory. Immatures lack complete breast-band of adults and somewhat resemble KENTISH PLOVER, but yellow legs and larger size distinguish them. Voice: liquid, rather melodious double note *'too-ee'* and during breeding season a trilling song.

Little Ringed Plover *Charadrius dubius*: 15 cm (6″) Summer visitor to region, north to southern Scotland and southern Scandinavia. Inhabits sandy or stony areas by fresh water, rarely found at coastal sites. More solitary than most plovers. Closely resembling RINGED PLOVER, smaller size rarely apparent in field. Differs in having orange eye-ring, **no white wing-bar** in flight, and smaller, less bulky head. Immatures have incomplete breast-band, somewhat resembling KENTISH PLOVER, but distinguished by pale legs and lack of wing-bar in flight. Voice: distinctive, high-pitched, rather piping *'tee-oo'*. Breeding-season song, series of disyllabic trilling notes.

Kentish Plover *Charadrius alexandrinus*: 15 cm (6″) Summer visitor to southern coast of North Sea and English Channel. Inhabits sandy and shingle beaches, and some dry mud areas. Paler, smaller, much slimmer bird than RINGED PLOVER, with much faster running and feeding action. Less black markings on face and **incomplete breast-band**. In flight shows white wing-bar and very conspicuous white sides to tail. **Black bill and legs** serve to distinguish from immature Ringed and LITTLE RINGED PLOVER. Voice: trilling song in breeding season, but call note distinctive, a single *'wit'* often repeated several times.

RINGED PLOVER

imm

ad

LITTLE RINGED PLOVER

ad

imm

15 cm (6 in.)

♀

♂

KENTISH PLOVER

PLOVERS (CHARADRIIFORMES; CHARADRIIDAE)

Grey Plover *Pluvialis squatarola*: 28 cm (11″)   Winter visitor to British Isles and coastal France, inhabiting mud-flats and river estuaries, rarely found inland. Resembles GOLDEN PLOVER, but occurs in different habitat. A plumper bird, heavier bodied with larger bill and eye. Upper-parts never show distinctive yellowish tinge of Golden Plover. In flight, **black under wings at the 'armpits'**, white rump, wing-bar and tail distinguish this species. Black-and-white breeding plumage unmistakable. Less likely to flock than Golden Plover, usually occurring as scattered individuals or small parties. Walks rather slowly when feeding, with hunched appearance. Voice: distinctive triple note, said to resemble a wolf-whistle.

Golden Plover *Pluvialis apricaria*: 28 cm (11″)   Summer visitor to Scandinavia, resident in British Isles except extreme south-east, winter visitor elsewhere in region. A bird of upland, moors and heaths, inhabiting farmland in winter and rarely visiting salt-water sites. Two races occur in region, but only separable in breeding plumage, the northern birds having greater expanse of black on under-part. Differs from similar-shaped GREY PLOVER in having all under-wing white, indistinct white wing-bar, and **rump and tail uniform with back**. In winter months found in large flocks, often mixed with LAPWINGS (p. 86), but smaller size, faster flight and pointed wings make them distinctive. Large flocks frequently perform aerial manoeuvres. When standing, often stretch wings above their backs. Voice: clear, rather liquid, single note, often extended to double note when alarmed. A trilling song on breeding ground.

Dotterel *Eudromias morinellus*: 22 cm (8·5″)   Summer visitor to mountainous and tundra areas of Scandinavia and Scotland, with small population on low-lying areas in Netherlands. Found in more open country and on shore while on migration. Very tame in breeding season, often allowing close approach, when distinctive breeding plumage is characteristic. In winter plumage, prominent **eye stripes almost meeting on nape of neck** and trace of pectoral band distinguish the species. In flight gives appearance of very stocky, short-tailed wader, with bright yellow legs often clearly seen. Female is slightly larger than male, latter undertaking incubation and rearing of young. Voice: soft twittering call often turning into rapid trill.

GREY PLOVER

winter

summer

northern race
summer

GOLDEN
PLOVER

southern race
summer

winter

DOTTEREL

winter

summer

15 cm (6 in.)

SANDPIPERS (CHARADRIIFORMES; SCOLOPACIDAE) *A widely varying group of basically long-billed and long-legged wading birds. Some species with distinctive breeding plumage. Sexes similar, immatures resemble adults in winter.*

Snipe *Gallinago gallinago*: 27 cm (10·5″) Summer visitor to central and northern Scandinavia, resident throughout rest of region. Inhabits damp and wet areas of farmland, marshes and moors. Well-camouflaged plumage makes bird difficult to see amongst vegetation, but is readily flushed. Characteristic **zigzag flight** is accompanied by harsh call, and **long bill** is carried downwards in distinctive manner. In breeding season has drumming display flight, said to resemble bleating of goat, when bird dives vertically, outer tail feathers extended to make vibrating noise. When alarmed, or with chicks, will often perch on low objects, persistently giving series of alarm calls. Readily flocks in winter months, small parties often performing aerial manoeuvres. Voice: harsh, scraping note in flight and persistent chipping alarm calls.

Great Snipe *Gallinago media*: 28 cm (11″) Summer visitor to Norway and northernmost Scandinavia, passage migrant through east of region. In breeding season inhabits marshy ground similar to SNIPE, but usually found in drier areas, such as farmland or heaths, in winter months and on migration. Slightly larger and heavier than Snipe, but differs in having barred under-parts, less white on belly, more white in tail and more distinctive white trailing edge to wing. **Flight is heavy and straight**, with bill proportionately shorter and held straighter. Usually silent or with weak croak when flushed. Has similar drumming display flight to Snipe. Voice: weak, croaking flight call and twittering or bubbling display 'song'.

Jack Snipe *Lymnocryptes minimus*: 19 cm (7·5″) Summer visitor to northernmost Scandinavia, winter visitor to France and British Isles, passage migrant in remainder of region. Inhabits similar areas to SNIPE but usually more muddy localities. Smaller than Snipe, with **short bill** and no white on tail. **Very difficult to flush**, often not rising until almost trodden upon when usually silent. Rarely flies great distances but drops quickly to ground. Has drumming display flight similar to other snipe but flight actions more varied and noise said to resemble galloping horse. Voice: generally silent.

Woodcock *Scolopax rusticola*: 34 cm (13·5″) Summer visitor to central Scandinavia, resident in south and remainder of region. **Inhabits woodland and heath**, feeding in slightly damper areas. Solitary, readily distinguished from snipe by habitat, large size and **rounded wings**. Flight rather heavy, often twisting amongst trees, appearing short-tailed and with bill pointing downwards. Most active at dusk and dawn, on breeding areas carrying out slow, distinctive display flight amongst trees. Voice: two distinct notes, one croaking and frog-like, the other sneezing or grunting.

SNIPE

GREAT SNIPE

JACK SNIPE

WOODCOCK

15 cm (6 in.)

SANDPIPERS (CHARADRIIFORMES; SCOLOPACIDAE)

Curlew *Numenius arquata*: 55 cm (22") Summer visitor to Scandinavia and east of region, resident or winter visitor elsewhere. Inhabits moors, heaths and grassland in breeding season, occurring in wetter areas during winter months, when regularly found on coastal sites, such as estuaries and mud-flats. Although somewhat variable in size, **largest white-rumped wader** of region, with distinctive **long, down-curved bill**. Highly characteristic voice. Forms large flocks in winter months, often flying in formation at considerable height. Voice: characteristic whistling *'curlee'*, often running into bubbling trill.

Whimbrel *Numenius phaeopus*: 41 cm (16") Summer visitor to Scandinavia and northernmost Scotland, passage migrant elsewhere in region. Inhabits highland moors and tundra. Smaller than CURLEW with distinctive **head markings** and shorter bill, much straighter at base. Flies with more agile flight and faster wing-beats. Often with Curlew on migration. Voice: short, twittering whistle rapidly repeated six or seven times.

Black-tailed Godwit *Limosa limosa*: 41 cm (16") Summer visitor to areas around southern North Sea, wintering from southern Britain westwards. Inhabits damp grassland in breeding season, occurring on estuaries and marshes in winter months. A tall-standing, long-billed wader with distinctive **black-and-white flight pattern**. Voice: wide variety of notes but commonest flight call *'weeka'* repeated three times.

Bar-tailed Godwit *Limosa lapponica*: 38 cm (15") Summer visitor to northernmost Scandinavia, wintering in coastal areas from southern Scandinavia westwards. Slightly smaller than BLACK-TAILED GODWIT, with more upturned bill and shorter legs, and feet not projecting beyond tail in flight. Summer plumage with reddish under-parts extending to tail, but at all times lacks striking black-and-white flight pattern. Winter flocks frequently perform aerial manoeuvres, unlike less acrobatic flight of Black-tailed Godwit. Voice: harsh, *'crick'* flight note.

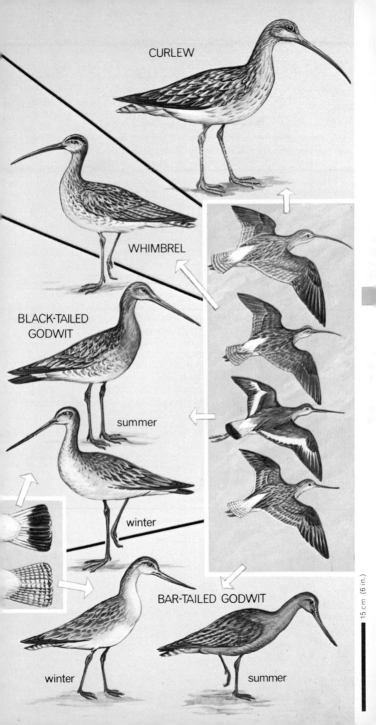

CURLEW

WHIMBREL

BLACK-TAILED GODWIT

summer

winter

BAR-TAILED GODWIT

winter

summer

15 cm (6 in.)

SANDPIPERS (CHARADRIIFORMES; Scolopacidae)

Green Sandpiper *Tringa ochropus*: 23 cm (9″) Summer visitor to southern Scandinavia, wintering from southern Britain southwards, passage migrant elsewhere in region. Inhabits wet woodland in breeding season, at other times mainly found by fresh water. Rather shy and usually solitary with **black-and-white appearance**, especially in flight, when black under-wing is apparent. Legs do not project beyond tail in flight, which is rather SNIPE-like (p. 92). Voice: when flushed has ringing, fluting, trisyllabic *'twee-twe-eet'*.

Wood Sandpiper *Tringa glareola*: 20 cm (8″) Summer visitor to Scandinavia, northern Scotland and northern Germany, passage migrant elsewhere in region. Inhabits fairly open upland areas near woods and water; on migration found almost entirely by fresh water. Differs from similar GREEN SANDPIPER in less black-and-white appearance with greyish under-wings, barred tail and yellowish **legs projecting beyond tail** in flight. On migration often in small noisy parties. Voice: a shrill *'chiff'* repeated three times.

Common Sandpiper *Tringa hypoleucos*: 20 cm (8″) Summer visitor throughout region, small numbers wintering in southern Britain and western France. Inhabits freshwater sites in upland areas, particularly fast-running streams. Occurs at any freshwater sites on migration. Solitary, less upright than WOOD or GREEN SANDPIPER, bobbing frequently when alarmed, and with distinctive flight pattern. Characteristic **flicking flight**, low over water with wings held bowed downwards. Often perches on low objects in water. Runs rapidly when feeding, when somewhat resembles stints (p. 102). Voice: rather shrill, musical three-noted whistle.

Spotted Sandpiper *Tringa macularia*: 20 cm (8″) Scarce North American visitor to region, closely resembling COMMON SANDPIPER; distinguished in summer months by black spots on under-parts and dark tip to yellow bill. In winter best distinguished by paler legs, barring on wing coverts and double, not treble, call note.

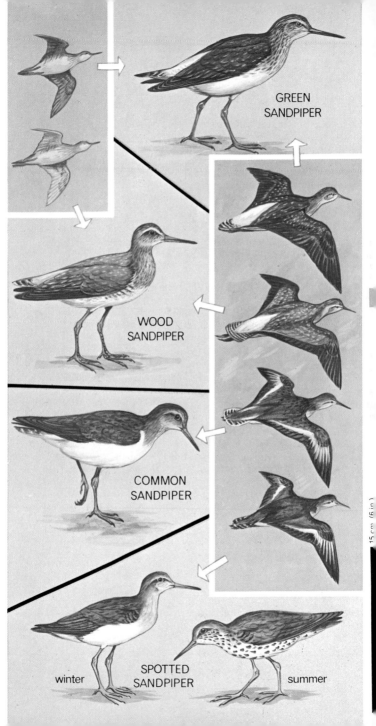

GREEN
SANDPIPER

WOOD
SANDPIPER

COMMON
SANDPIPER

winter   SPOTTED
SANDPIPER   summer

15 cm (6 in.)

SANDPIPERS (CHARADRIIFORMES; SCOLOPACIDAE)

Redshank *Tringa totanus*: 28 cm (11″) Summer visitor to Scandinavia and east of region, resident in British Isles, passage migrant or winter visitor elsewhere. Inhabits wet areas, sometimes with dense ground vegetation. Occurring in more open, muddy, estuary sites in winter months. An obvious species, **easily disturbed**, when bobs or jerks tail readily. Perches freely on posts or exposed objects on breeding grounds. During fast flight with jerky wing-beats has conspicuous **white trailing edge to wing** and white rump. Readily flocks in winter. Voice: high-pitched series of yelping or whistling notes and musical song in flight on breeding grounds.

Spotted Redshank *Tringa erythropus*: 30 cm (12″) Summer visitor to northernmost Scandinavia, wintering in southern Britain and western France, passage migrant elsewhere. In breeding season inhabits damp, open areas of forest, occurring in more coastal exposed sites in winter months. Dark summer plumage unmistakable with contrasting white rump extending up back. In winter, paler than REDSHANK, lacking white markings on wings. Larger, slimmer bird than Redshank with longer bill and legs, often wading body-depth in water. In flight, feet trail well beyond tail. Usually solitary. Voice: drawn-out whistling *'chew-wit'*.

Lesser Yellowlegs *Tringa flavipes*: 25 cm (10″) Scarce, but annual vagrant to region from North America. Smaller and more delicate than REDSHANK, appearance somewhat resembling WOOD SANDPIPER (p. 96). Yellow legs and feet, clearly visible beyond tail in flight, and white rump not extending up back. Pale superciliary stripes meet on forehead. Voice: up to three soft whistling *'chu'* notes.

Greenshank *Tringa nebularia*: 30 cm (12″) Summer visitor to Scandinavia and northernmost Scotland, wintering in western Britain and France, passage migrant elsewhere. Found in marshes, moors and forests, never far from water. Outside breeding season occurring mainly at freshwater sites. Larger and paler than REDSHANK, with longer, upturned bill, greenish legs and paler, whiter face. In flight has no wing-bar and white of rump extends well up back. Usually solitary, or in small parties. Voice: typical flight note three short whistling *'chu-chu-chu'*.

SPOTTED REDSHANK

REDSHANK

winter

summer

LESSER
YELLOWLEGS

GREENSHANK

15 cm (6 in.)

SANDPIPERS (CHARADRIIFORMES; SCOLOPACIDAE)

NORTH AMERICAN WADERS Species on this page, together with SPOTTED SANDPIPER (p. 96) and LESSER YELLOWLEGS (p. 98), are the more regular of North American vagrant waders to occur in western Europe. When seen, they are often in company with more familiar species of the region.

Pectoral Sandpiper *Calidris melanotos*: 19 cm (7·5") Inhabits drier areas than many waders on migration, rarely found on sea-shore. Between DUNLIN (p. 102) and KNOT (p. 104) in size with rich brown upper-parts, streaked with paler lines. Sharply marked division between streaked breast and pure white under-parts. Flight rather SNIPE-like (p. 92) with zigzag pattern when first flushed. Often stretches neck to give tall, thin appearance when alarmed. Voice: rather low single or double '*trrrp*'.

White-rumped Sandpiper *Calidris fuscicollis*: 18 cm (7") Occurs on marshes and beaches. Small, stint-like (p. 102) wader with short, thin, straight bill. In flight shows indistinct wing-bar on rather long wings. White rump, narrower than that of larger CURLEW SANDPIPER (p. 102). Voice: thin characteristic '*jeeet*'.

Buff-breasted Sandpiper *Tryngites subruficollis*: 20 cm (8") Inhabits dry fields and short-grass areas, rarely found on shore. Somewhat resembles RUFF (p. 106) but smaller, with shorter bill and unpatterned upper-parts in flight when white wing-linings contrast with rufous under-parts. Often tame. Voice: low trilling call.

Long-billed Dowitcher *Limnodromus scolopaceus*: 30 cm (12") Usually found in freshwater areas with associated vegetation. Bulky bird somewhat resembling large SNIPE (p. 92) with long bill but in flight white rump extends well up back. Very similar, but much rarer Short-billed Dowitcher, *Limnodromus griseus*, has slightly shorter bill, wings projecting beyond tail when perched, and spotted, not barred, flanks. Very rapid feeding action, thrusting long bill vertically into mud. Voice: long, shrill, repeated '*keeek*'.

PECTORAL
SANDPIPER

WHITE-RUMPED
SANDPIPER

BUFF-BREASTED
SANDPIPER

LONG-BILLED
DOWITCHER

winter

summer

15 cm (6 in.)

SANDPIPERS (CHARADRIIFORMES; SCOLOPACIDAE)

Little Stint *Calidris minuta*: 13 cm (5″) Spring and autumn migrant throughout region, inhabiting marshes and mud-flats often in mixed parties with other small waders. **Smallest of the common waders.** Rather like miniature DUNLIN with short, straight bill. **Feeds and runs rapidly**, actively picking from surface of mud. In winter plumage looks pale around head, with white breast, upper-part strongly marked with V pattern of white, very obvious in immatures. In flight shows white sides to rump but **no white in tail.** Legs black. Voice: sharp, short, single *'chit'* note.

Temminck's Stint *Calidris temminckii*: 14 cm (5·5″) Summer visitor to northern Scandinavia, migrant through eastern parts of region in small numbers west as far as eastern Britain. Inhabits more freshwater sites than LITTLE STINT, particularly vegetated areas. Only rarely found on sea-shore. Similar to Little Stint in build and size, resembling miniature COMMON SANDPIPER (p. 96). Differs from Little Stint in having more **uniform grey appearance** with a complete **pectoral breast-band, white outer tail feathers** and greenish-yellow legs. When flushed often towers upwards in flight, resembling SNIPE (p. 92). Voice: distinctive short trilling note.

Dunlin *Calidris alpina*: 18 cm (7″) Present throughout year in northern Britain and southern Scandinavia, summer visitor to northern Scandinavia, winter visitor or passage migrant throughout remainder of region. Breeds in damp areas of upland, moors and heaths; outside breeding season the com-monest small wader of the sea-shore. Feeding flocks present a rather distinctive hunched appearance, large concentrations often performing aerial manoeuvres. In summer plumage the only wader with **black belly patch**, while in winter generally much greyer, with white under-parts. Voice: rather weak flight note *'chreep'*.

Curlew Sandpiper *Calidris ferruginea*: 19 cm (7·5″) Passage migrant to the region, mainly in autumn, numbers varying greatly from year to year. Inhabits similar areas to DUNLIN, with which frequently consorts. Distinctive reddish summer plumage, in winter months paler than Dunlin with strong, **superciliary stripe.** Longer legged than Dunlin. **Distinctive white rump** in flight, all other white-rumped waders having a straight bill. General appearance of a rather long-necked small wader standing very upright. Voice: soft liquid chirping note.

winter

summer   LITTLE
STINT

summer

TEMMINCK'S
STINT

winter

summer

DUNLIN

winter

CURLEW
SANDPIPER

summer

winter

15 cm (6 in.)

SANDPIPERS (CHARADRIIFORMES; SCOLOPACIDAE)

Knot *Calidris canutus*: 25 cm (10″)   Winter visitor to east of region, passage migrant elsewhere. Inhabits coastal sites, feeding on exposed mud at low tide when highly gregarious, large flocks often tightly packed together. A relatively short-billed dumpy wader appearing reddish in summer and very grey and uniform in winter. In flight shows **uniform grey rump and tail** and no striking flight pattern. Large flocks often perform aerial manoeuvres involving rapid twists and turns low over the mud. Voice: quiet, low *'nutt'*.

Purple Sandpiper *Calidris maritima*: 21 cm (8″)   Present throughout year in north Scandinavian coastal areas, in winter south to English Channel and west to Ireland, confined to rocky shores and islands. Rarely in large numbers, usually in small parties mixed with TURNSTONES (p. 86). Presents a rather stocky, round appearance, often very tame. A rather **dark wader** with white throat and eye-ring, yellow base to bill and **yellow legs** often visible at some distance. Voice: low short piping note.

Broad-billed Sandpiper *Limicola falcinellus*: 16·5 cm (6·5″) Summer visitor to northern Scandinavia, passage migrant through east of region. Breeds in wet upland areas, occurring in muddy, often inland sites on migration, rarely met on sea-shore. Solitary, seldom mixing with other waders, appearing as a small dark DUNLIN (p. 102) but with white belly in summer. Very short legs and long bill, heavy at base, decurved at tip. **Snipe-like** (p. 92) **markings on back and head**. Very inactive compared with other small waders. Voice: low trill and double flight note.

KNOT

summer

winter

PURPLE
SANDPIPER

summer

winter

BROAD–BILLED
SANDPIPER

15 cm (6 in.)

SANDPIPERS (CHARADRIIFORMES; Scolopacidae)

Ruff *Philomachus pugnax*: Male 29 cm (11·5"); female 23 cm (9") Summer visitor to Scandinavia and coastal areas of southern North Sea, wintering in southern Britain and western France, passage migrant elsewhere in region. Breeds in wet grassland and marshes, inhabiting freshwater sites in winter and on migration. Rarer in coastal waters. In flight has dark centre to **rump with white oval patches on each side**. General sandy coloration and scaly upper-parts. Male in breeding plumage unmistakable. In winter appears rather uniform, thinnish-necked, tall wader with relatively short bill, pale forehead and yellowish or reddish legs. Female, or reeve, much smaller and rather thinner in appearance. Not very gregarious, usually in small parties and not associated with other waders. Voice: generally silent, but has low, guttural, rather grating flight call.

STILTS (CHARADRIIFORMES; Recurvirostridae) *Distinctive long- and thin-legged, long-billed black-and-white waders.*

Avocet *Recurvirostra avosetta*: 43 cm (17") Summer visitor to coastal areas of southern North Sea and eastern England, small numbers wintering in south-west Britain and western France. Inhabits estuaries and salt marshes at coastal sites and also inland. Rarely found by fresh water. Unmistakable, the only black-and-white wader with an **upturned bill** which is used for feeding by sweeping from side to side in shallow water. Distinctive flight pattern with legs trailing well beyond tail. Voice: very vocal, soft grunting flight call or loud yelping notes.

Black-winged Stilt *Himantopus himantopus*: 38 cm (15") Summer visitor to some isolated sites in south of region. Inhabits marshes and pools, both fresh and salt water. Unmistakable, the only black-and-white wader with **long, thin, pink legs** and fine, needle-like black bill. Both upper- and under-surface of wings black. In flight long legs trail well behind tail. Voice: series of 'cic-cic-cic' notes.

STONE CURLEWS (CHARADRIIFORMES; Burhinidae)

Stone Curlew *Burhinus oedicnemus*: 41 cm (16") Summer visitor to east of region from southern Britain southwards. Inhabits generally dry, open areas of stony heath and farmland. Often secretive and difficult to observe as generally crepuscular or nocturnal. Presence in area often established by distinctive voice at night. If flushed, flight usually slow and direct, low over ground. Yellow eye, yellow base to bill and yellow legs often distinctive coupled with **striking wing pattern**. Usually solitary or in pairs, but family parties form flocks in autumn. Voice: series of bubbling liquid call notes, at times resembling Curlew (p. 94) but more varied.

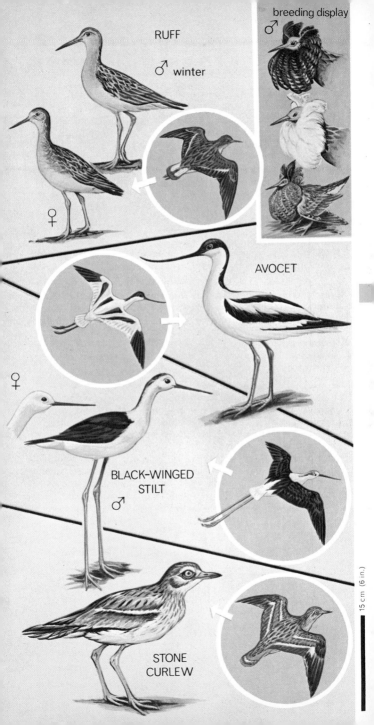

breeding display

♂

RUFF

♂ winter

♀

AVOCET

♀

BLACK-WINGED
STILT

♂

STONE
CURLEW

15 cm (6 in.)

SANDPIPERS (CHARADRIIFORMES; SCOLOPACIDAE)

Sanderling *Calidris alba*: 20 cm (8″)   Winter visitor to coastal areas from southern North Sea westwards, passage migrant elsewhere. Inhabits sandy shores, rarely occurring elsewhere. Slightly larger and plumper than DUNLIN (p. 102), with which often associated. Easily identified in winter plumage by **general white appearance** and feeding habit of chasing backwards and forwards with each wave. In summer more reddish in coloration but with white belly and under-tail, retaining typical feeding movements on **rapidly-moving black legs**, feeding with short, all-black bill. Often runs rather than flies when approached. In flight has very conspicuous broad white wing-bar. Voice: single short, sharp '*wic*' flight note.

PHALAROPES   (CHARADRIIFORMES;   PHALAROPODIDAE)

Small, tame marine waders, very white in winter plumage with distinctive summer plumage. Females brighter than males. Readily swim, often spinning rapidly round in circles while picking insects from the surface. Inhabit open seas in winter.

Grey Phalarope *Phalaropus fulicarius*: 21 cm (8″)   Sometimes occurs in autumn and winter in western coastal areas as far east as southern North Sea, usually after severe westerly weather. Summer plumage distinctive. Differs from RED-NECKED PHALAROPE by having **short, rather stout bill** and in winter by thicker neck and more uniform grey back. Voice: low, quick '*wit*'.

Red-necked Phalarope *Phalaropus lobatus*: 18 cm (7″) Summer visitor to northern Scandinavia and northern Britain, passage migrant elsewhere in region. Breeds beside pools or areas of wet marshes. On migration frequently encountered at freshwater sites. Less inclined to swim than GREY PHALAROPE, and rarely encountered in mid-winter. Summer plumage distinctive. Differs from Grey Phalarope in having **thin, needle-like bill**, and in winter by more black-and-white appearance and patterned back, with thinner neck and more upright stance. Flight faster, more buoyant than Grey Phalarope, sometimes resembling SWALLOW (p. 156). Voice: similar to Grey Phalarope but also grunting call.

SANDERLING

summer

winter

summer ♀

summer ♂

pinning(both species)

GREY PHALAROPE

winter ♂ & ♀

summer

summer ♂

♀

winter ♂ & ♀

15 cm (6 in.)

RED-NECKED PHALAROPE

SKUAS (CHARADRIIFORMES; STERCORARIIDAE) *Dark, gull-like sea-birds, most species showing light wing-patches at base of primaries and elongated central tail feathers. Often occur in two distinct phases, light and dark. Feed by chasing other sea-birds until they drop or disgorge their food. Sexes similar, immatures lighter, more scaly than adults.*

Great Skua *Stercorarius skua*: 58 cm (23″)   Breeds in northern Scotland, occurring elsewhere in region in coastal localities of British Isles and western France. Nests in scattered colonies in coastal moorland sites. Marine outside breeding season, inhabiting open seas for much of winter. Largest and heaviest of the skuas with short tail and **very prominent white wing flashes**. Flight agile, particularly when chasing, but heavier than gull with broad, rather rounded wings. Bill heavy and strongly hooked. Readily settles on water. Voice: deep guttural flight call.

Pomarine Skua *Stercorarius pomarinus*: 51 cm (20″)   Occurs in coastal localities throughout region as passage migrant. Larger than ARCTIC SKUA with heavier flight and deeper-breasted appearance. Adults have characteristic **blunt and twisted central tail feathers**. Immatures differ from Arctic Skua in having rather heavier build and broader bases to pointed wings, very mottled upper-parts and slightly yellowish barring on under-parts. The light phase commoner than dark phase. Voice: double gull-like yelp, said to sound like '*which-you*'.

Arctic Skua *Stercorarius parasiticus*: 46 cm (18″)   Summer visitor to coastal areas of Scandinavia and northern Scotland. Outside breeding season occurs in coastal sites throughout region. Nests in colonies on coastal, moorland and tundra sites. **Commonest skua** of region with graceful and buoyant flight but hawk-like and dashing when chasing. Many variations and intermediates between light and dark phases occur, but light-phase birds commoner in more northern colonies. Smaller and slighter of build than POMARINE SKUA with more slender bill and narrower base to wings. Voice: high-pitched, rather squealing double note.

Long-tailed Skua *Stercorarius longicaudus*: 51 cm (20″), but not including 12–26 cm (5–10″) of central tail-feather projection. Summer visitor to northern Scandinavia, elsewhere occurs as passage migrant throughout coastal areas of region. Breeds in upland tundra sites in scattered colonies. Smallest and most graceful of the skuas with **extremely long central tail feathers** and much whiter under-parts. Generally greyer and less dark brown. Immatures are less bulky than ARCTIC SKUA with smaller bill and less white in the wing. Unlike other skuas swims with neck stretched and tail cocked. Voice: high-pitched, drawn-out note.

GREAT SKUA

light phase

dark phase

POMARINE SKUA

ad

imm

ARCTIC SKUA

imm

ad

light phase

dark phase

imm

ad

LONG-TAILED SKUA

15 cm (6 in.)

GULLS (CHARADRIIFORMES; LARIDAE) *Familiar sea-birds, although some species frequently well inland. Very gregarious. Plumage shows white below and various shades of white to black above. Scavengers, rarely diving for food. Colonial nesting. Sexes similar, immatures mainly brown, acquiring adult plumage after two to five years.*

Ivory Gull *Pagophila eburnea*: 44 cm (17·5″)   Winter visitor to extreme far north of Scandinavia. Inhabits the high Arctic, frequenting the edges of pack ice. The smallest **pure white gull** of region with **short black legs**. Small headed and plump, making it appear dove-like. Flight is tern-like (p. 124) with long wings, buoyant and graceful. Rarely settles on water. Very distinctive immature plumage has patterns of black on white. Voice: harsh double or single tern-like note.

Great Black-backed Gull *Larus marinus*: 70 cm (27·5″) Present in coastal areas throughout region, breeding on rocky sea cliffs and islands, rarely inland. Largest dark-backed gull of region, with massive **squarish head**, **thick neck** and **heavy bill** giving cruel appearance. Highly predatory on other birds and mammals. Back and wings uniformly dark, but see Scandinavian race of LESSER BLACK-BACKED Gull. Legs flesh pink. Less colonial than other gulls, single pairs often nesting amongst other species. Flight heavy, wing-beats slow and wings very broad. Voice: harsh deep yelping and chuckling notes.

Lesser Black-backed Gull *Larus fuscus*: 54 cm (21″)   Summer visitor to Scandinavia and northern and western Britain, wintering or passage migrant throughout remainder of region. Inhabits coastal areas but frequently seen inland when on migration. Breeding colonially on islands, beaches and upland areas. Similar to GREAT BLACK-BACKED GULL but distinguished by smaller size, more **narrow wings**, smaller bill, **rounded head** and **yellow legs**. In flight shows more extensive area of black on under-side of wings. Two races occur; in west of region with paler back and wing coverts contrasting with blacker flight features. Birds from Scandinavia have uniform black back and wings (see Great Black-backed Gull). Immatures very similar to immature HERRING GULL (p. 114) but generally darker on the wings. Voice: similar to Herring Gull but slightly deeper in tone.

IVORY GULL

ad

imm

ad

GREAT
BLACK-BACKED
GULL

imm

sub-ad

ad

ad

ad

sub-ad

imm

LESSER
BLACK-BACKED
GULL

15 cm (6 in.)

GULLS (CHARADRIIFORMES; LARIDAE)

Herring Gull *Larus argentatus*: 61 cm (24″) Present in all coastal areas throughout year, frequently inland during winter months. Breeds in variety of marine sites from islands, cliffs and dunes to roof-tops of coastal towns. In winter inhabits wide range of sites from rubbish dumps to grass fields. **Commonest** and most widespread **gull** of the region. Frequently follows ships and regularly uses up-currents from cliffs or buildings for soaring and gliding. The similar COMMON GULL (p. 116) is smaller and slighter built. Immatures similar to immature LESSER BLACK-BACKED GULL (p. 112) but generally slightly paler on wing. Voice: wide variety of laughing and yelping cries.

Glaucous Gull *Larus hyperboreus*: 76 cm (30″) Winter visitor to coastal regions of Scandinavia, British Isles and southern North Sea, inhabiting open beaches and harbours, very rare inland. Largest of all the pale gulls of the region but rather variable in size. Complete **lack of black on wing-tips**. Build similar to GREAT BLACK-BACKED GULL (p. 112) with **heavy head and bill** and thick neck. Flight heavy, appearing rather slow, with broad, rather rounded wings giving bird an owl-like silhouette. Behaviour resembles Great Black-backed Gull. Hybrids with HERRING GULL frequently occur. Voice: similar to Herring Gull.

Iceland Gull *Larus glaucoides*: 56 cm (22″) Winter visitor to northern and western areas of British Isles. Inhabits coastal sites usually mixing with parties of other large gulls. Differs from the similar GLAUCOUS GULL in having **small head, thin neck** and less heavy bill, giving bird a rather COMMON GULL (p. 116) appearance to the head. Tips of rather long **wings project well beyond tail**. Flight more buoyant than Glaucous Gull with more rapid wing-beats. Voice: resembles Herring Gull.

HERRING GULL

imm sub-ad ad

ad

ad

imm

GLAUCOUS GULL

ad

sub-ad

ad

imm

ad

ICELAND GULL

15 cm (6 in.)

GULLS (CHARADRIIFORMES; Laridae)

Common Gull *Larus canus*: 41 cm (16″) Summers through-out Scandinavia and northern Britain with isolated breeding sites further south. Found in coastal areas throughout region in winter, occurring inland on migration. Breeds in wide variety of coastal sites and also by fresh water inland. Resembles a rather small HERRING GULL (p. 114) but with finer bill and rather **delicate-looking head**. Differs from somewhat similar KITTIWAKE (p. 118) in having rounder head with **yellow-green legs** and white spots on black wing-tips. Flight graceful, wings appearing long with rounded ends. Voice: resembles rather weak, high-pitched Herring Gull.

Mediterranean Gull *Larus melanocephalus*: 39 cm (15″) Winter visitor to western coast of France with isolated breeding populations on the English Channel coast. Inhabits coastal areas often associated with BLACK-HEADED GULL. Build and shape resemble COMMON GULL rather than Black-headed Gull, but stockier appearance with white wing-tips and heavier **bill with rather drooping appearance**. Longer legged than Black-headed Gull. Immature plumage more black and white than Common Gull with narrower tail-band. Sub-adults have uniform back and wing coverts. Voice: resembles rather deep call of Black-headed Gull.

Black-headed Gull *Larus ridibundus*: 37 cm (14·5″) Resi-dent throughout region from southern Scandinavia south-wards. Inhabits wide variety of sites, nesting in marshes, islands, beaches, etc. and wintering in both coastal and inland sites on farmland and waste ground. Common around towns in winter. The most familiar of the smaller gulls of the region. Frequently follows the plough when feeding in farmland areas. Flight strong and rather tern-like (p. 124), very buoyant. The only gull to show **white leading edges to the outer wing feathers in all plumages**. Voice: very vocal when nesting, with harsh, raucous cries.

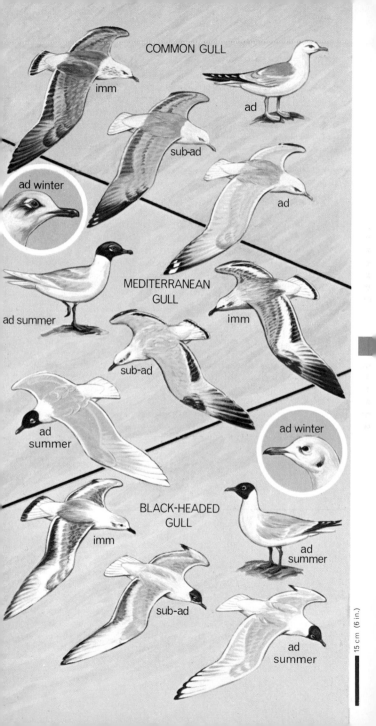

COMMON GULL

imm

sub-ad

ad

ad winter

ad

MEDITERRANEAN
GULL

ad summer

imm

sub-ad

ad
summer

ad winter

BLACK-HEADED
GULL

imm

sub-ad

ad
summer

ad
summer

15 cm (6 in.)

GULLS (CHARADRIIFORMES; LARIDAE)

Little Gull *Larus minutus*: 28 cm (11") Summer visitor to isolated breeding areas in southern Scandinavia and southern North Sea. Winter visitor or migrant further west. Inhabits marshes and freshwater sites, occurring in coastal localities on migration or during winter. Smallest, most tern-like (p. 124) gull of region, with buoyant, graceful flight resembling BLACK TERN (p. 120); when feeding picks food from surface of water. **No black wing-tips** on short rounded wings. Adults show **black under-wings**. Distinctive wing patterning of the immature resembles larger KITTIWAKE, but lacking slightly forked tail. Voice: sharp, trisyllabic call.

Sabine's Gull *Larus sabini*: 33 cm (13") Passage migrants to marine sites in extreme west of region. Rather scarce in coastal waters. Small and tern-like (p. 124). Only gull of region with a **markedly forked tail**. Strongly patterned upper-surface of the adult in flight is distinctive. Flight graceful, bouncing and tern-like, feeding from surface of water. Usually seen singly, when behaviour resembles LITTLE GULL. Voice: tern-like grating note.

Kittiwake *Rissa tridactyla*: 41 cm (16") Marine species throughout region, visiting sea cliffs and occasionally coastal buildings for breeding in Scandinavia, British Isles and north-west France. Very rare inland. Somewhat similar to COMMON GULL but differs in having less round head, short black legs and **no white in black wing-tips**. Immatures have similar patterning to immature LITTLE GULL but differ in size, heavier flight and having slightly forked tail. Regularly follows ships. Buoyant flight distinctive at some distance when rather broad, pale trailing edge to wing gives a definite **narrow-winged effect**. Voice: very vocal on breeding cliffs with distinctive '*kitty-waak*'.

LITTLE GULL

imm

ad

ad summer

ad winter

SABINE'S GULL

imm

ad

ad summer

ad winter

KITTIWAKE

imm

ad

ad

ad

15 cm (6 in.)

TERNS (CHARADRIIFORMES; LARIDAE) *Graceful, slender birds, less marine and more specialized than gulls. Pointed, dagger-like bills, short legs and forked tails. Sea terns are generally whitish with black caps and feed by diving into water. Marsh terns have generally darker overall plumage and feed by picking from surface of water while in flight. Sexes similar, winter plumage less clear-cut, immatures resembling adults in winter.*

Black Tern *Chlidonias niger*: 24 cm (9·5") Summer visitor to region, north to south-east Britain and southern Scandinavia. Nests almost exclusively on vegetation floating in shallow water areas. Commonest of the marsh terns with graceful but erratic flight sweeping and dipping above surface of water. Never dives. Occasionally feeds over dry land on migration, often in large flocks. **In winter** plumage has **distinctive black shoulder-mark**. Voice: usually silent but has short, sharp 'kic kic'.

White-winged Black Tern *Chlidonias leucopterus*: 24 cm (9·5") Summer visitor to isolated breeding sites in east of region. Inhabits similar areas to BLACK TERN with which it often associates. Summer plumage distinctive. In winter, distinguished from Black Tern by shorter, more stubby bill, lack of dark shoulder-mark, **white rump** and white, less forked tail. Immatures show strongly contrasting back and wings. Flight less erratic than Black Tern. Voice: similar to, but harsher than, Black Tern.

Whiskered Tern *Chlidonias hybrida*: 25 cm (10") Summer visitor to south of region and isolated breeding sites in coastal areas of southern North Sea. Largest of the marsh terns, in some ways resembling a rather dark COMMON TERN (p. 124) and will dive for food in addition to feeding in manner of BLACK TERN. Immature has mottled mantle and darker rump than WHITE-WINGED BLACK TERN. In winter lacks dark shoulder-patches and less black on crown than Black Tern. **Bill longer and deeper than other marsh terns**. Voice: rasping disyllabic calls.

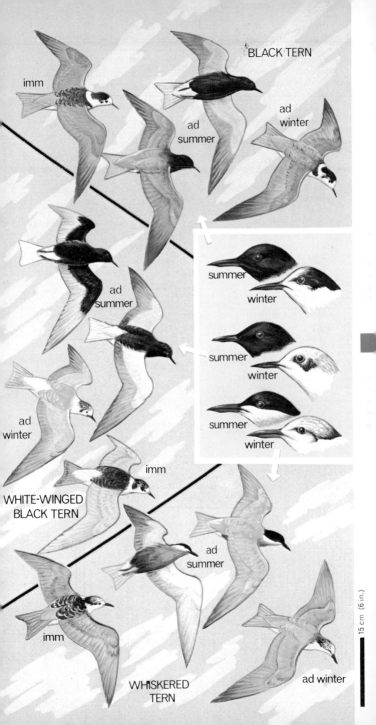

BLACK TERN

imm

ad summer

ad winter

ad summer

ad winter

imm

WHITE-WINGED BLACK TERN

summer
winter

summer
winter

summer
winter

ad summer

imm

ad winter

WHISKERED TERN

15 cm (6 in.)

TERNS (CHARADRIIFORMES; LARIDAE)

Gull-billed Tern *Gelochelidon nilotica*: 38 cm (15″) Summer visitor to extreme south of Scandinavia and isolated coastal sites in southern North Sea. Closely resembles SANDWICH TERN, but more an inhabitant of fresh water; hawks for food over land and water, rarely diving. Differs from Sandwich Tern in being greyer, particularly on rump and tail which is less forked. Has broader wings giving rather gull-like flight and short, **stubby, heavy, all-black bill**. Shorter neck, giving stouter appearance, and when perched, longer legs distinctive. Voice: characteristic double or treble '*ker-ak*'.

Caspian Tern *Hydroprogne caspia*: 53 cm (21″) Summer visitor to Baltic coast of Scandinavia. Chiefly inhabits coastal sites but also occurs on freshwater and inland localities. Largest tern of the region, approaching HERRING GULL (p. 114) in size, with **huge red bill**. Very gull-like in general appearance and regularly settles on water, often behaving like gulls with scavenging diet, but principally dives for fish. Characteristic dark under-sides to primaries. Voice: deep, gruff, crow-like call.

Sandwich Tern *Sterna sandvicensis*: 41 cm (16″) Summer visitor to British Isles, southern Scandinavia, and coastal areas of southern North Sea and English Channel. Found exclusively in coastal sites, very rare inland. Breeds in large, closely packed, very noisy colonies. Largest of the common terns of the region, with slim, elegant, very white and long-necked appearance. Only tern with long **yellow-tipped black bill** and crested effect on nape. Immatures often lack yellow-tipped bill making confusion possible with GULL-BILLED TERN, but whiter appearance, more elongated shape, graceful flight and short legs. Voice: very vocal, distinctive '*kirrick*'.

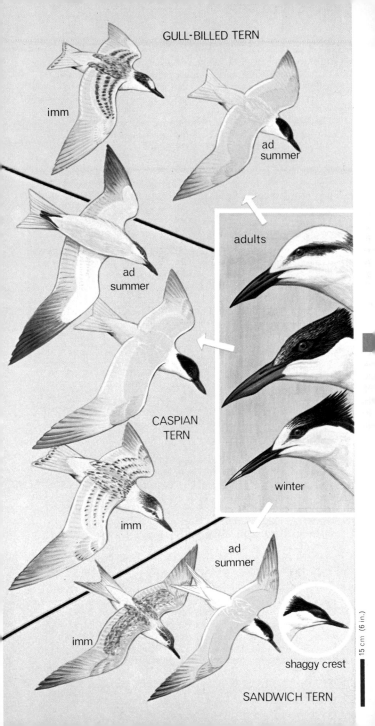

GULL-BILLED TERN

imm

ad
summer

adults

ad
summer

CASPIAN
TERN

winter

imm

ad
summer

imm

shaggy crest

SANDWICH TERN

15 cm (6 in.)

TERNS (CHARADRIIFORMES; LARIDAE)

Common Tern *Sterna hirundo*: 35 cm (14") Summer visitor throughout region except northernmost Scandinavia, mainly inhabiting coastal sites but also breeding inland near fresh water. With the three somewhat similar species, Common, ARCTIC and ROSEATE TERN, identification can be difficult. Common Tern is the most numerous and widespread species of region, with wing-tips and tail-tip level in standing adults, and upper-parts greyer than Roseate Tern, but tending to lack the extensive grey on under-parts of Arctic Tern. Bill length between the other two species, in summer crimson with black tip. Immatures show extensive brown markings on body and around head. Only **inner flight feathers show translucency** when viewed against light. Adult birds tend to keep their red legs in winter. Voice: very striking and carrying double note '*kee-yah*', and a persistent '*kic-kic-kic*'.

Arctic Tern *Sterna paradisaea*: 35 cm (14") Summer visitor to coastal localities from English Channel northwards, extending further north than COMMON TERN, only exceptionally occurring inland. Wing-tips extend slightly beyond tail-tip in standing adult when very short legs noticeable. Adults rather greyer than Common Tern, particularly on under-parts. Bill shorter and finer than other two species, completely blood-red in summer, becoming all dark in winter. Immatures lack brown markings on body and have narrow, sharply defined black leading edge to wing. **All flight feathers show translucency** when viewed against light, clearly edged with narrow black tippings to feathers. Often mixes with Common Terns and most easily separated when both species present for comparison. Voice: similar to Common Tern but said to have rising inflection.

Roseate Tern *Sterna dougallii*: 38 cm (15") Summer visitor to British Isles and north-west France. Almost entirely coastal, very rare on fresh water. Very long tail-streamers extending well beyond tail-tip of standing adult. In all plumages **appears strikingly white** on both upper- and under-parts and in breeding adults distinctive pink flush to under-parts. In summer, bill dark with deep red base, becoming all dark in winter. Immatures tend to have more extensive dark cap and finely marked with black on body and wings. In flight all wing feathers appear translucent when viewed against light. Flight more buoyant and with shallower wing-beats than other two species. Voice: a distinctive call, a double '*chu-wic*'.

Little Tern *Sterna albifrons*: 24 cm (9·5") Summer visitor to coastal sites of region north to northern Britain and southern Scandinavia. Almost exclusively coastal, inhabiting shingle or sandy beaches. Smallest tern of region. Very rapid wing-beats, regularly hovering before diving for food. At all times very active. Head markings, yellow bill and leg colour characteristic. Voice: distinctive note a persistent '*kip-kip-kip*'.

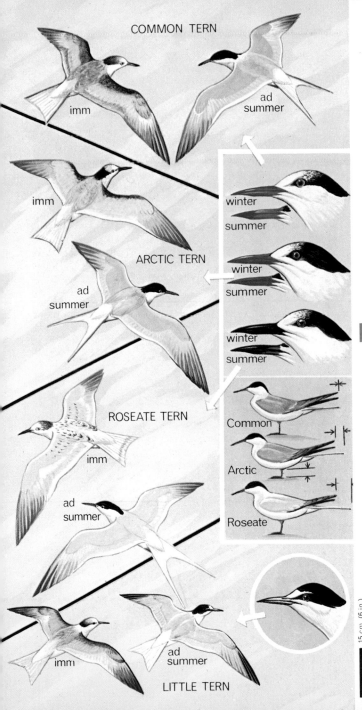

COMMON TERN

imm

ad
summer

winter
summer

winter
summer

winter
summer

Common

Arctic

Roseate

ARCTIC TERN

imm

ad
summer

ROSEATE TERN

imm

ad
summer

LITTLE TERN

imm

ad
summer

15 cm (6 in.)

AUKS (CHARADRIIFORMES; ALCIDAE) *Sea-birds appearing black above and white below with a general penguin-like appearance, diving from the surface for food. Very small wings with whirring flight. Upright stance on legs at rear of body. Sexes similar, winter plumage generally whiter.*

Razorbill *Alca torda*: 40 cm (16") Inhabits coastal cliffs throughout region, becoming highly marine in winter months. Swims and dives readily with shuffling gait on land but only comes ashore to breed unless oiled or storm driven. Body plumage blacker than similar GUILLEMOT with **distinctively shaped bill** showing white line, also white line between bill and eye. Appears less elongated than Guillemot with shorter, broader bill and thicker neck. Usually swims with tail in more cocked position. Voice: variety of whistling and growling notes when breeding.

Guillemot *Uria aalge*: 41 cm (16") Inhabits rocky coastal sites throughout region becoming highly marine in winter. Rare on shore outside breeding season. The commonest auk of the region, generally browner than RAZORBILL but some northern birds tend to be darker. More slender than Razorbill with longer, **pointed bill** and longer, thinner neck. Tail appears shorter in flight. The northern colonies have proportion of the 'bridled' phase with white eye-ring and white line extending backwards from eye. In winter plumage dark line extending backwards from eye is distinctive. Behaviour as Razorbill. Voice: rather shrill whistling notes on breeding ground.

Brünnich's Guillemot *Uria lomvia*: 42 cm (16·5") Winter visitor to northernmost Scandinavia. Probably impossible to distinguish from GUILLEMOT except on close view. Has a rather shorter, stouter bill than Guillemot with white line near base. In winter plumage black of crown extends well below eye. Tends to be more oceanic than Guillemot. Habits, flight and voice similar to Guillemot.

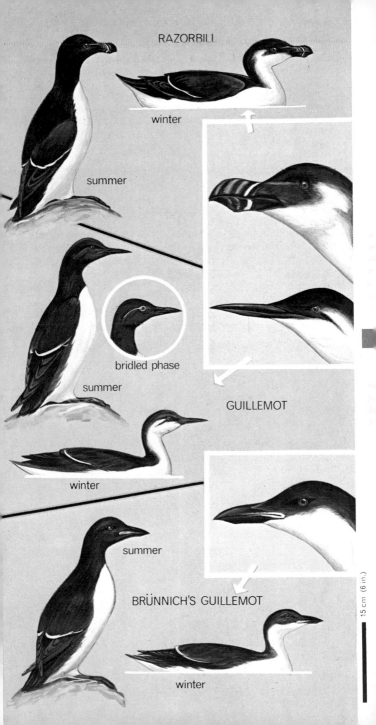

RAZORBILL

winter

summer

bridled phase

summer

winter

GUILLEMOT

summer

BRÜNNICH'S GUILLEMOT

winter

15 cm (6 in.)

AUKS (CHARADRIIFORMES; ALCIDAE)

Little Auk *Plautus alle*: 20 cm (8″) Winter visitor to marine areas of northern Britain and western Scandinavia. Rarely comes to land except after severe storms when individuals sometimes appear well inland. Smallest auk of the region, near STARLING (p. 208) in size, and sometimes appearing like a very small pigeon. The **smallest diving sea-bird**, with tubby appearance, lacking neck with very short bill. At sea flocks fly in extended line low over water. Voice: high-pitched chattering.

Black Guillemot *Cepphus grylle*: 34 cm (13·5″) Resident in coastal regions of Scandinavia, northern Britain and Ireland, small numbers moving south in North Sea during winter. Inhabits shallow seas around rocks and cliffs. Less communal than other auks, often breeding singly or in small colonies. The most distinctively plumaged of the auks, basically **black in summer** and **white in winter**. Flight very low over water, with rapid wing-beats. Behaviour similar to GUILLEMOT. Voice: rather weak, high-pitched twittering.

Puffin *Fratercula arctica*: 30 cm (12″) Summer visitor to coastal sites of British Isles, western Scandinavia and north-western France. Marine in winter. Inhabits grass-covered islands or cliffs. Breeding plumage distinctive. Stout body and short neck with rounded head and **conical bill** give a very large-headed appearance in flight. Sits higher on water than other auks when swimming. Voice: usually silent but series of growling notes at breeding ground.

LITTLE AUK

summer

winter

BLACK GUILLEMOT

winter

summer

summer

imm

PUFFIN

winter

15 cm (6 in.)

PIGEONS and DOVES (COLUMBIFORMES; COLUMBIDAE)
*Plump greyish or brownish birds with small heads, short bills
and longish tails. Walk easily on the ground. All species have
cooing calls. Sexes, winter and summer plumages similar.*

Stock Dove *Columba oenas*: 33 cm (13″)   Summer visitor to
southern Scandinavia and eastern Germany, resident throughout remainder of region. Inhabits open woodland areas or more
open sites with scattered trees or old buildings. More frequent
on farmland outside breeding season. Rather uniform,
lacking any white markings. Often in mixed parties with
WOODPIGEONS when smaller size and more rapid wing-beats
aid identification. In display, flies with gliding, circular pattern
on raised wings. Behaviour very like Woodpigeon. Voice:
grunting, double cooing note.

Rock Dove *Columba livia*: 33 cm (13″)   Resident on coastal
cliffs of northern and western Britain and north-western
France. The wild ancestor of the domestic pigeon and distribution of truly wild birds now difficult to establish. Most
characteristic plumage markings are two black wing-bars and
white rump. Almost always in small flocks. Smaller, neater
than WOODPIGEON, with faster, more active flight. Voice:
similar to domestic pigeon.

Woodpigeon *Columba palumbus*: 41 cm (16″)   Summer visitor
to central Scandinavia, resident through remainder of region.
Inhabits woodland country, feeding on open farmland
throughout the year. In recent years a considerable extension
in habitat, birds becoming familiar in towns, parks and
gardens. Commonest, largest and most widespread of the
pigeons, often in vast flocks. **White neck and wing-marks**
distinctive. Flight fast and direct, often crashing out of trees
with wing-clapping. Characteristic display flight flapping
upwards then gliding down with wings raised above body.
Often tame in towns but very wary in rural areas. Voice:
series of cooing notes '*cooo, coo, coo-coo, cu*'.

STOCK DOVE

ROCK DOVE

feral Rock Doves

ad

imm

WOODPIGEON

15 cm (6 in.)

PIGEONS and DOVES (COLUMBIFORMES; COLUMBIDAE)

Turtle Dove *Streptopelia turtur*: 27 cm (11") Summer visitor north to England and southern Scandinavia. Inhabits parks, gardens, open woodlands with scattered trees, orchards, etc. Slimmer than other pigeons with faster, more direct flight and jerky wing action. Wing-clapping and gliding during display flight. Darker and smaller than similarly built COLLARED DOVE with **distinctive tail pattern**. Usually occurs in pairs or small flocks. Voice: soft purring notes.

Collared Dove *Streptopelia decaocto*: 30 cm (12") Resident throughout region north to southern Scandinavia, but spreading north-westwards in recent years. Very much associated with man, inhabiting towns and villages, often feeding around grain stores or poultry farms. Larger, more uniform in appearance than TURTLE DOVE, approaching STOCK DOVE (p. 130) in size. Distinctive **broad white-tipped tail**. Flight less jerky than Turtle Dove, often very tame. Young birds can closely resemble the domesticated Barbary Dove, *Streptopelia risoria,* a smaller bird, only 25 cm (10") in length, which often escapes from captivity. It differs from the Collared Dove in having paler, more creamy plumage and lacks black, contrasting flight feathers and grey coloration in the tail. Voice: persistent, monotonous, triple cooing note.

TURTLE DOVE

COLLARED DOVE

ad

imm

Barbary Dove

ad

imm

15 cm (6 in.)

BARN OWLS (STRIGIFORMES; Tʏᴛᴏɴɪᴅᴀᴇ)

Barn Owl *Tyto alba*: 35 cm (14″)   Resident throughout region except central and northern Scandinavia. Inhabits open country with scattered trees and buildings. Apart from sɴᴏᴡʏ ᴏᴡʟ, the palest owl of the region, appearing all white in flight. The only owl with a **heart-shaped face pattern**. Usually nocturnal but during summer months often hunts at dusk quartering low over ground on rather long wings. Frequently seen in headlights of cars, when appears very white. When alarmed lowers head and waves body slowly from side to side. The dark-breasted race occurs in the eastern parts of the region. Voice: variety of hissing and screeching notes.

OWLS (STRIGIFORMES; Sᴛʀɪɢɪᴅᴀᴇ)   *Mainly nocturnal birds of prey with large rounded heads and forward-looking eyes set in facial disc. Silent flight. Some species with feathered tufts on head. Sexes similar.*

Eagle Owl *Bubo bubo*: 69 cm (27″)   Resident in south-east Germany and throughout Scandinavia, except far north. Inhabits dense forests and rocky country on mountainsides. One of the largest owls of the region although rather uncommon. **Large feather tufts** set well apart **on head**. Female slightly larger than male. Hunts at dawn and dusk for largish mammals and birds, spending day in tree, usually near trunk, or deep crevices in rocks. Always solitary. Voice: far-carrying, very deep *'boo-hoo'*.

Snowy Owl *Nyctea scandiaca*: Male 53–58 cm (21–23″); female 58–66 cm (23–26″)   Resident in northern Scandinavia and Scotland. Inhabits moorland and open tundra. Largely diurnal and solitary. **Very white** and **round headed**. Female more strikingly marked with black. Flight includes much gliding and somewhat resembles ʙᴜᴢᴢᴀʀᴅ (p. 60) but dashes rapidly when swooping on to prey. Regularly settles on ground or sits in exposed position. Feeds largely on lemmings, many birds moving south and west at times of food shortage. Voice: usually silent but barking notes when breeding.

white-breasted
race

BARN OWL

dark-breasted
race

EAGLE OWL

♂

♀

SNOWY OWL

♀

15 cm (6 in.)

OWLS (STRIGIFORMES; STRIGIDAE)

Scops Owl *Otus scops*: 20 cm (8″)   Summer visitor to south of region. Inhabits wide variety of areas, usually with scattered trees, often near human habitation. Only completely migratory owl of the region. **Small size** and **feather tufts on head** distinctive, although tufts not always apparent. Occurs in two colour phases, brown and grey. Slimmer, less rounded body than slightly larger LITTLE OWL but head more rounded, less flattened. Rather long wings which reach tip of longish tail. Often sits in stretched, elongated position. Highly nocturnal. Flight more direct than Little Owl. Feeds mainly on insects. Voice: soft, monotonous, regularly repeated *'peehw'*, sometimes continued throughout night.

Pygmy Owl *Glaucidium passerinum*: 16 cm (6·5″)   Resident throughout most of central Scandinavia. Inhabits mountainous, dense coniferous woodlands. **Smallest owl of region**, appearing rather small headed and with indistinct facial disc but rather strongly marked short white brows above eye. Short, wide tail is flicked or jerked upwards regularly. Very active and aggressive, hunting small birds in flight both by day and night. Flight strongly undulating, resembling LITTLE OWL. Voice: variety of whistling and piping notes.

Little Owl *Athene noctua*: 22 cm (8·5″)   Resident in region north to southern Scotland and southern Scandinavia. Occurs in wide variety of habitat from farmland and open country to woodland, orchards and treeless areas. Most familiar of the small owls of the region with **flattened head shape** and short tail. Active both day and night, regularly sitting on exposed fence posts or similar perch. When alarmed bobs body and moves head from side to side. Flight low, strongly undulating, and will hover when hunting. Voice: loud, far-carrying *'kiu'* and variety of short barking notes.

Tengmalm's Owl *Aegolius funereus*: 25 cm (10″)   Resident throughout most of Scandinavia and extreme east of region. Inhabits dense coniferous forests in upland or mountainous areas. Completely nocturnal owl with rounded head and strongly marked facial disc with broad, **white**, **raised eyebrows**. Very upright stance. Flight wavers from side to side rather than undulating. Voice: series of whistling notes said to resemble the sound of dripping water.

SCOPS OWL

brown phase

grey phase

PYGMY OWL

LITTLE OWL

imm

TENGMALM'S OWL

15 cm (6 in.)

OWLS (STRIGIFORMES; STRIGIDAE)

Hawk Owl *Surnia ulula*: 38 cm (15″) Resident throughout central and northern Scandinavia inhabiting coniferous forests and woodland areas of mountains and tundra. Regularly diurnal, often perching in exposed position on top of tree, with **long tail** often held cocked or raised and lowered slightly. Short, rather **pointed wings** give hawk-like outline. Flight direct and fast including gliding, and will hover, often sweeping upwards to perch. Aggressive in behaviour. Voice: chattering series of hawk-like (p. 62) notes.

Great Grey Owl *Strix nebulosa*: 69 cm (27″) Resident in northernmost Scandinavia. Inhabits coniferous forests. Similar in size to EAGLE OWL (p. 134) but basically grey coloration with **large rounded head**, no feather tufts on head, and long tail. Largely diurnal, hunting for medium-sized mammals. Voice: resembles Tawny Owl (p. 140).

Ural Owl *Strix uralensis*: 61 cm (24″) Resident throughout much of central and eastern Scandinavia. Inhabits a variety of woodland sites mainly in upland areas. Slightly smaller than similar GREAT GREY OWL, somewhat resembling a large, pale TAWNY OWL (p. 140) with long tail. Differs from Great Grey Owl in having dark eyes and **unmarked facial disc** with shorter and narrower wings. Longish tail hangs down in flight. Often active in daylight, hunting medium-sized birds and mammals. Voice: variety of barking and harsh notes similar to Tawny Owl.

HAWK OWL

GREAT GREY OWL

URAL OWL

15 cm (6 in.)

OWLS (STRIGIFORMES; STRIGIDAE)

Tawny Owl *Strix aluco*: 38 cm (15″) Resident throughout region except northernmost Scandinavia and Ireland. Inhabits variety of mixed and open deciduous woodland, large gardens, parks and towns. Commonest and most familiar owl of the region. Strongly nocturnal, if seen in daylight usually roosting close to trunk of tree where frequently mobbed by smaller birds. Large, round headed, differing from similar-sized LONG-EARED OWL by lack of feather tufts on head. General coloration variable, usually brown but a less common grey phase also occurs. Voice: barking '*kerwic*' and familiar hooting rendered as '*too-wit, too-woo*'.

Long-eared Owl *Asio otus*: 36 cm (14″) Resident throughout region except northernmost Scandinavia where summer visitor in some areas. Principally inhabits coniferous forests but also occurs in more open areas on migration and hunts in open country. Highly nocturnal. **Elongated facial disc** and long feather tufts on head. Can elongate body when sitting to appear very thin. Longer winged and tailed than TAWNY OWL, which it otherwise resembles in basic outline. Flies with deep slow wing-beats. When feeding young in nest often hunts at dusk. Voice: drawn-out moaning hoot; distinctive hunger call of young sounds like creaking hinge.

Short-eared Owl *Asio flammeus*: 38 cm (15″) Summer visitor to central and northern Scandinavia, elsewhere resident or winter visitor. Inhabits open moorlands and downs including heath and marshes. **Active in daylight**, the only medium-sized brown owl likely to be seen by day, regularly sitting on ground or exposed open perch. Short feather tufts on head are rarely visible. Hunts in manner of harriers (p. 64), quartering low over ground with slow, steady flaps of rather long wings, and dropping on to prey. Wings frequently held in raised position when gliding. Wing-clapping occurs during display flight. Usually solitary, but occasionally in small parties outside breeding season. Voice: barking note in flight.

TAWNY OWL

grey phase

LONG-EARED OWL

SHORT-EARED OWL

15 cm (6 in.)

CUCKOOS (CUCULIFORMES; CUCULIDAE)

Cuckoo *Cuculus canorus*: 33 cm (13″) Summer visitor throughout region. Inhabits wide variety of areas, ranging from woodland and farmland to open upland sites, towns and parks. Probably best known for its **distinctive song**. In flight wings do not come above level of body. Flight direct, usually low and only gliding before perching. The long tail of the flying bird suggests SPARROWHAWK (p. 62) but the pointed wings and thin bill distinctive. The rufous phase of the female is rather rare. Solitary. Often mobbed by smaller birds, especially during breeding season. Voice: characteristic *'coc-oo'*, while female has far-carrying bubbling note.

NIGHTJARS (CAPRIMULGIFORMES; CAPRIMULGIDAE)

Nightjar *Caprimulgus europaeus*: 27 cm (10·5″) Summer visitor throughout region except northernmost Scandinavia. Inhabits open woodlands, heaths and forest edges. Nocturnal, most active soon after dusk when presence often detected by churring song. Unlikely to be seen in daylight when perfectly camouflaged while sitting on ground or perched along branch. If flushed almost underfoot, rather **long winged** and **long tailed** and gives impression of bird of prey or CUCKOO. Very large gape for catching insects in flight when very erratic and silent, although during breeding season claps wings to make cracking note. Voice: persistent churring with occasional changes in pitch. Quiet, clicking flight note.

KINGFISHERS (CORACIIFORMES; ALCEDINIDAE)

Kingfisher *Alcedo atthis*: 17 cm (6·5″) Resident throughout region except Scotland, central and northern Scandinavia. Inhabits most low-lying freshwater sites although occasionally moves to coastal areas in winter months. Highly distinctive plumage. Very rapid, direct, usually low flight with very fast wing-beats, the bird appearing as a flash of blue. **Feeds by diving for fish** from perch or after hovering. Usually solitary. Very short tailed and when perched regularly 'bobs' head and tail. Voice: very loud and shrill *'keee'*.

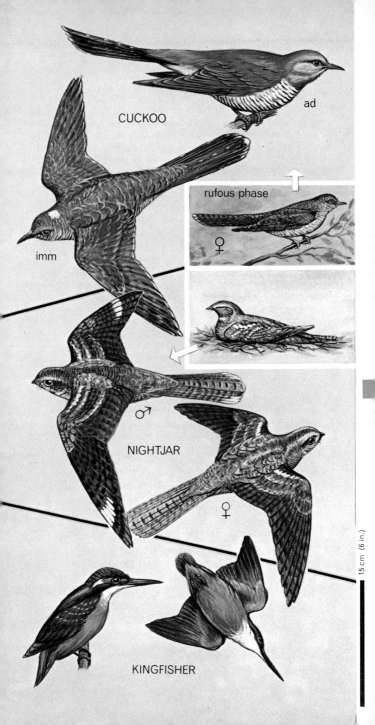

CUCKOO

ad

imm

rufous phase

♀

NIGHTJAR

♂

♀

KINGFISHER

15 cm (6 in.)

SWIFTS (APODIFORMES; APODIDAE) *Highly specialized aerial-living birds, somewhat similar to swallows and martins (p. 156) but longer, thinner winged. Generally dark brown plumage and appearing to have sickle-shaped wings beating alternately. Sexes, winter and summer plumages similar.*

Swift *Apus apus*: 16·5 cm (6·5″)   Summer visitor throughout region except northernmost Scandinavia. Being principally aerial can occur anywhere, feeding over freshwater sites and breeding around buildings and cliff faces. Very sociable. **All-dark swift**, with barely noticeable white throat. Flight highly active, often wheeling and chasing between buildings but will circle apparently rather leisurely at great height. During breeding season very vocal parties often chase one another around nesting areas. Large movements often take place before summer thunderstorms. Voice: harsh screaming cries.

Alpine Swift *Apus melba*: 21 cm (8·5″)   Summer visitor to extreme south of region. Inhabits rocky and cliff sites in rather high or mountainous areas. Very sociable. Larger and paler than SWIFT, with fatter body and distinctive **white belly and chin**. Often mixes with Swift when larger size and 53–cm (21″) wing-span very apparent. Wing-beats rather slower than Swift, but flight faster. Behaviour and flight similar to Swift, but when gliding wings frequently held below horizontal. Voice: distinctive whistling trill.

BEE-EATERS (CORACIIFORMES; MEROPIDAE)

Bee-eater *Merops apiaster*: 28 cm (11″)   Rather scarce summer visitor to extreme south of region. Inhabits open country, usually sandy areas, with small numbers of trees or low bushes often near water. An **unmistakable brightly coloured** bird with rather long, slightly decurved bill and **projecting central tail feathers**. Very sociable, parties often perching in exposed areas particularly favouring wires. Feeds on flying insects by making highly manoeuvrable flights from perch, returning in the manner of flycatchers (p. 198). Flight rather martin-like (p. 156), with triangular wings and much gliding. Voice: distinctive, very liquid *'kwilp'* flight note.

SWIFT

Swift

Swallow

House Martin

ALPINE SWIFT

imm

ad

BEE-EATER

15 cm (6 in.)

ROLLERS (CORACIIFORMES; CORACIIDAE)

Roller *Coracias garrulus*: 30 cm (12″)   Summer visitor to extreme south-east of region. Inhabits open areas of well-wooded country with a proportion of old rotten trees. Basically **blue, crow-sized bird**, in some ways reminiscent of JAY (p. 162). Bird's name derived from the breeding display flight with rolling and tumbling action. Normal flight direct, pigeon-like with rapid wing-beats, but shape of bird crow-like. Regularly sits on exposed perches, dropping to ground for prey, such as beetles and lizards, in the manner of a shrike (p. 206). Moves on ground with heavy hopping action. Voice: crow-like '*cra-ak*' and series of chattering notes.

HOOPOES (CORACIIFORMES; UPUPIDAE)

Hoopoe *Upupa epops*: 28 cm (11″)   Summer visitor north to English Channel coast, occasional migrant birds appearing in southern Scandinavia, southern Britain and Ireland. Inhabits wide variety of open countryside and parklands with trees and buildings, particularly favouring orchards and vine-yards, often very close to human habitation. Unmistakable. Crest can be erected or depressed, usually raised when alarmed or when alighting from flight. Feeds on ground favouring close-cropped grass where runs rapidly, stopping to probe with decurved bill. Will perch readily on bushes, rocks and buildings. **Flight undulating**, opening and closing **very rounded wings** in woodpecker-like (p. 148) action. Voice: rapid, far-carrying '*who-who-who*' and series of chattering notes when alarmed.

ORIOLES (PASSERIFORMES; ORIOLIDAE)

Golden Oriole *Oriolus oriolus*: 24 cm (9·5″)   Summer visitor north to southern Scandinavia and English Channel coast. Inhabits well-wooded parks and gardens and deciduous forests. Unmistakable but difficult to observe; **very secretive, more often heard than seen,** keeping high in tree canopy. Rare at ground level except when bathing. Usually solitary. Sometimes confused with GREEN WOODPECKER (p. 148) but general shape very different although undulating flight similar. Distinctive upwards sweep at end of flight to regain tree canopy. Voice: distinctive fluty whistling '*weela-weo*' said to recall its name '*or-i-ole*', and series of squawking notes, rather cat-like.

ROLLER

HOOPOE

displaying

GOLDEN ORIOLE

♀

♂

15 cm (6 in.)

WOODPECKERS (PICIFORMES; PICIDAE) *Strictly wood-land species, highly adapted to climbing amongst trees, probing for food in wood and excavating holes in rather rotten wood for nesting. Two toes pointing forwards and two backwards for clinging to tree-trunks and stiff tail feathers to act as support. Always progress upwards. Very undulating flight. Several species make mechanical 'drumming' noise by hammering on wood. Sexes, summer and winter plumages similar but males usually with more extensive red on head.*

Black Woodpecker *Dryocopus martius*: 46 cm (18″)   Resident throughout Scandinavia and extreme east of region. Inhabits mainly coniferous forests but sometimes found in mixed woodland areas. **Largest woodpecker** of region, size of crow (p. 158) and equally **all black** although males with red crown and females with red patch on back of head. Longer necked than other woodpeckers giving characteristic head shape when perched. Flight very undulating, rare on ground. Voice: drums with longer, louder phrases than other species, loud string of double or treble vocal notes often used in flight.

Green Woodpecker *Picus viridis*: 33 cm (13″)   Resident throughout region except northern Scandinavia, northernmost Scotland and Ireland. Inhabits all types of wooded country but favours deciduous or mixed forests. **Commonest woodpecker** of the region, only similar species is GREY-HEADED WOODPECKER from which it differs in having darker head and neck and more extensive head markings. **Regularly comes to ground** where hops in ungainly upright position and feeds on lawns or open areas, particularly visiting ant-hills. Very undulating flight, wings closed for long periods between each period of flapping. Voice: rarely, if ever, drums, series of loud yelping cries and laughing, ringing triple call.

Grey-headed Woodpecker *Picus canus*: 25 cm (10″)   Resident in central Scandinavia and extreme east of region extending westwards into central France. Habitat similar to GREEN WOODPECKER but usually at higher altitudes where the ranges of the two species overlap. Rather similar in appearance to larger Green Woodpecker but generally less numerous. Differs in having **grey head and neck** and lack of extensive red on crown and much narrower moustachial markings. Behaviour as Green Woodpecker. Voice: drums regularly (unlike Green Woodpecker). Calls similar to Green Woodpecker but slower, less ringing and tending to fade away.

BLACK
WOODPECKER

♂

♀

♀

GREEN
WOODPECKER

♂

♀

♂

imm

♂

♀

imm

GREY-HEADED
WOODPECKER

15 cm (6 in.)

WOODPECKERS (PICIFORMES; PICIDAE)

Great Spotted Woodpecker *Dendrocopos major*: 23 cm (9″)
Resident throughout region except northernmost Scandinavia
and Ireland. Inhabits wide variety of wooded country including mixed forests and conifers, as well as scattered gardens
and parks, sometimes close to the centre of towns. **Commonest black-and-white woodpecker** of region. Prominent
white patches on wings are distinctive, only other species
with these marks is the smaller MIDDLE SPOTTED WOODPECKER
which has extensive red on crown. Immatures differ from
Middle Spotted Woodpecker in having more black on face and
larger white shoulder-patches. Strongly undulating flight
giving very bounding appearance, rarely comes to ground.
Increasing habit of visiting bird-tables for food and attacking
tops of milk bottles in suburban areas. Voice: drums frequently and rapidly for short periods. Far-carrying *'tcicc'*
and various churring notes.

White-backed Woodpecker *Dendrocopos leucotos*: 25 cm
(10″) Resident in central Scandinavia. Inhabits deciduous
woodlands always with a high proportion of dead or rotting
trees. Uncommon. Largest black-and-white woodpecker of
region with a less bulky appearance than other species and
longer bill. Distinguished by prominent **white barring on
wings** and **white rump**. Voice: drumming consists of a
series of single blows, call notes like quiet Great Spotted
Woodpecker.

Middle Spotted Woodpecker *Dendrocopos medius*: 22 cm
(8·5″) Resident from southern Scandinavia and English
Channel southwards. Inhabits deciduous and mixed woodland
areas. Differs from GREAT SPOTTED WOODPECKER in smaller
size, and having gap between black cheek-mark and nape,
and all-red crown (but immature Great Spotted Woodpecker
has red crown). Usually shows extensive **pink on under-
parts**. Very active, tends to stay high in tree canopies.
Voice: drums less frequently than Great Spotted Woodpecker,
call is a series of sharp, single notes.

GREAT SPOTTED
WOODPECKER

♂

♀

imm

WHITE-BACKED
WOODPECKER

♂ ♀

imm

MIDDLE SPOTTED
WOODPECKER

15 cm (6 in.)

WOODPECKERS (PICIFORMES; PICIDAE)

Three-toed Woodpecker *Picoides tridactylus*: 22 cm (8·5″)
Resident in central and northern Scandinavia. Inhabits coniferous woods with a proportion of old trees but in far north also
found in deciduous woodland. Rather uncommon but very
distinctive black-and-white woodpecker, with mainly **black
wings** and **white back from nape to rump**. Never shows
any red in plumage. Head appears large and dark compared
with other black-and-white woodpeckers. Less active than
other woodpeckers but flies faster and less undulatingly.
Voice: drums rather slowly and infrequently, call notes
resemble a soft Great Spotted Woodpecker (p. 150) but less
vocal than other woodpeckers.

Lesser Spotted Woodpecker *Dendrocopos minor*: 14 cm (5·5″)
Resident throughout region except northern Scotland and
Ireland. Inhabits mixed and deciduous woodlands and more
open sites such as parks, large gardens, etc. **Smallest woodpecker** of the region with distinctly **barred plumage**.
Larger THREE-TOED WOODPECKER is the only other black-and-
white woodpecker to lack red under tail. Shy and elusive,
usually found high up in trees amongst the smaller branches
and in winter months will join mixed tit (p. 164) flocks for foraging. Appears to flutter among the branches but flight in open
has characteristic woodpecker undulations although slower
than other species. Voice: drums regularly, quieter but for
longer periods than Great Spotted Woodpecker. Call notes
consist of a series of soft ringing notes and quiet Great Spotted
Woodpecker-type '*cick*'.

Wryneck *Jynx torquilla*: 16·5 cm (6·5″)   Summer visitor north
to southern England and central Scandinavia, migrants appearing regularly on east coast of Britain and southern Ireland.
Inhabits rather open deciduous woodland and areas of
scattered trees such as orchards, large gardens, etc. General
appearance unwoodpecker-like with long-tailed appearance
in flight and large warbler-like (p. 186) stance. Crown feathers
erectile. Rather shy and easily overlooked. Flight more direct
than woodpeckers', less undulating, when tail-bands and
grey rump often conspicuous. Regularly comes to ground
where very active, hopping with tail raised. Often **perches
along branches** rather than across, and has ability to cling to
tree-trunks like woodpecker. Can turn head through strange
angles from which is derived the bird's name. Voice: does not
drum; ringing, clear, musical series of notes, rather reminiscent
of bird of prey.

THREE-TOED
WOODPECKER

♂

♀

LESSER SPOTTED
WOODPECKER

♂

♀

15 cm (6 in.)

crest erected

WRYNECK

LARKS (PASSERIFORMES; ALAUDIDAE) *Ground-living birds of open country with strong legs and stoutish bills. Generally streaked brown, resembling pipits (p. 200) but shorter tailed, stouter bodied and broader winged. Song usually from flight. Sexes, summer and winter plumages generally similar.*

Short-toed Lark *Calandrella cinerea*: 14 cm (5·5″) Summer visitor to south-west of region. Inhabits open country. Smaller, paler than SKYLARK with patch on side of neck; clear, **unstreaked under-parts**. Display flight rising and falling. Winter flocks tame, when disturbed fly close to ground. Centre of tail looks black in flight. Voice: sparrow-like chirping and musical song.

Crested Lark *Galerida cristata*: 17 cm (6·5″) Resident southern Scandinavia and English Channel southwards. Inhabits wide variety of sites. Differs from SKYLARK by larger **crest**, **always erect**, and **buff outer feathers of** shorter **tail**. Plumper than Skylark with less strongly marked upper-parts. Lacks white trailing edge to wings. Flight undulating and irregular giving unco-ordinated appearance. Rarely flocks in winter when often tame. Voice: song lacking variety; frequently uttered from perch or ground. Call, a whistling, trisyllabic rising and falling.

Woodlark *Lullula arborea*: 15 cm (6″) Summer visitor to east of region; elsewhere resident north to southern England. Inhabits open meadow and heathland with scattered trees. Distinguished from SKYLARK by **short tail** with white tips to outer feathers. **Superciliary stripes meet on nape**. Markings on leading edge of wing not easily seen. Undulating, jerky flight, often perches on trees or wires. Forms small flocks in winter months. Voice: song, delivered from circular flight pattern, fluty and musical, descending the scale, often at night. Flight call rich, bubbling and musical.

Skylark *Alauda arvensis*: 18 cm (7″) Resident north to southern Scandinavia, summer visitor to central Scandinavia. Inhabits grassland, heaths and cultivation. **Most familiar lark of region**; white outer feathers to longish tail and **white trailing edge to wing**. Walks with hunched appearance, crouches when alarmed, jumping into flight when disturbed. Large flocks in winter. Voice: warbling song when rising, falling and hovering; liquid chirping call.

Shore Lark *Eremophila alpestris*: 16·5 cm (6·5″) Summer visitor to central and northern Scandinavia, wintering in coastal zones of southern North Sea. During breeding season inhabits rocky and open areas at high altitudes. **Distinctive head and face pattern**. Very active on ground, running at considerable speed. Flight more undulating than other larks. Small flocks in winter often mixing with SNOW BUNTINGS (p. 224). Voice: song rather Skylark-like, usually from ground. Call similar to Yellow Wagtail (p. 204).

SHORT-TOED LARK

neck spot

CRESTED LARK

buff under wings

wing edge

WOODLARK

song flight

SKYLARK

ad summer

SHORE LARK

imm & winter

15 cm (6 in.)

SWALLOWS (PASSERIFORMES; HIRUNDINIDAE) *Slim, graceful birds adapted for aerial living, long winged and forked tailed (except Crag Martin), legs and bill short, bill wide. Often in large flocks, many breeding in colonies. Sexes, winter and summer plumages similar.*

Swallow *Hirundo rustica*: 19 cm (7·5″) Summer visitor to region except northernmost Scandinavia. Inhabits wide variety of sites, associated with water but usually nesting around buildings. **Commonest** and most familiar **swallow of region**. Settles readily on buildings, wires, bushes, trees, etc.; rarely landing on ground except when collecting mud for nest. Graceful flight, frequent changes of direction when hawking for insects but flight more direct when migrating. After breeding season forms large communal parties, often roosting together with martins in reed-beds. Voice: twittering, rather repetitive song and frequent short, twittering flight call.

Red-rumped Swallow *Hirundo daurica*: 18 cm (7″) Southern European species of rather rare occurrence but occasionally appearing during summer months in more southern parts of the region. Usually found near buildings, bridges, etc., often near the centre of towns. Differs from SWALLOW by **capped appearance**, reddish nape and rump. Slower, less agile flyer than Swallow. Voice: less musical song than Swallow and rather harsh, drawn-out flight note.

Crag Martin *Hirundo rupestris*: 15 cm (6″) Summer visitor to extreme south of region; inhabits cliffs and buildings, often near towns. Rather scarce and local, appearing as **large, dark, chunky** SAND MARTIN with broader wings and square tail. Differs in having **brownish under-parts** and no prominent breast-band. White tail spots only visible on close examination. Voice: weak twittering song and flight call.

House Martin *Delichon urbica*: 13 cm (5″) Summer visitor throughout region; inhabits wide variety of sites, frequently associated with human habitation, nesting on buildings, etc., also occurs on cliffs and rocky areas. Distinguished by **prominent white rump**. Tail shorter, less forked than RED-RUMPED SWALLOW. Behaviour similar to SWALLOW but more communal, nesting in colonies. Flight more direct than Swallow but wing action less purposeful. Voice: quiet twittering song usually delivered in flight; sharp, high-pitched alarm note.

Sand Martin *Riparia riparia*: 12 cm (4·75″) Summer visitor throughout region, inhabiting wide variety of areas near water, nesting often in large colonies in holes excavated in sandbanks. **Smallest swallow** of region with distinctive **breast-band on white under-parts**. Seen almost exclusively over water with very erratic flight action and rarely gliding. After breeding season often roosts communally in large numbers in reed-beds, etc. Voice: twittering flight call uttered persistently to form song.

SWALLOW

imm

RED-
RUMPED
SWALLOW

imm

CRAG MARTIN

HOUSE MARTIN

SAND MARTIN

15 cm (6 in.)

CROWS (PASSERIFORMES; CORVIDAE) *Largish, generally dark or black perching birds with harsh cries. Longish, stout bills. Often highly gregarious. Sexes, autumn and winter plumage similar.*

Raven *Corvus corax*: 63 cm (24″) Resident throughout Scandinavia, northern and western Britain and some coastal areas of continental Europe. Inhabits open and upland areas from sea cliffs and moors to mountains. **Largest** all-black **crow** of region, with massive bill and **wedge-shaped tail**. More likely to soar than other crows when appears long necked. Spring flight includes much acrobatics as part of display. Extremely wary, usually seen singly or in small parties at food source such as a carcass. Very successful scavenger. Voice: deep, gruff croaking.

Carrion Crow *Corvus corone corone*: 46 cm (18″) Resident throughout region except Scandinavia and Ireland. Inhabits wide variety of areas but favours farmland and woodland. Differs from HOODED CROW (a geographical race of the same species) by all-black plumage although hybrids with varying plumages between the two do occur. Differs from similar-sized all-black ROOK (p. 160) in deeper, heavier bill and less ragged wing-tips in flight, **greenish-blue gloss** to plumage and **lack of 'trousered' effect**. Bill feathered to base (but see immature Rook). Usually seen **singly or in pairs** but family parties and small flocks do occur in winter months. Rather laboured flight, rarely soaring, with ungainly hopping and walking when on ground. Frequently feeds by dropping hard-cased food, such as nuts and shellfish, from a height. Voice: rasping deep croak, often repeated two or three times.

Hooded Crow *Corvus corone cornix*: 46 cm (18″) Summer visitor to northernmost Scandinavia, resident in remainder of Scandinavia, northern and western Britain. Winter visitor throughout rest of region. Geographical race of the CARRION CROW and where the two races meet as breeding birds numerous intermediates with variable plumages occur. Habits, habitat and voice resemble Carrion Crow.

RAVEN

CARRION CROW

HOODED CROW

15 cm (6 in.)

CROWS (PASSERIFORMES; CORVIDAE)

Rook *Corvus frugilegus*: 46 cm (18″)   Resident throughout region north to southern Scandinavia. Inhabits open farmland with scattered trees or woods. Differs from similar sized and coloured CARRION CROW (p. 158) by **purple gloss** to plumage, **shaggy 'trousered' appearance**, more ragged look in flight, and in adult by **bare face**. Immatures feathered to base of bill but usually with white throat-patch. Bill thinner and less heavy than Carrion Crow. Highly gregarious, often in huge flocks mixed with JACKDAWS. Nests communally in tree-tops. Feeding birds have slow, precise walk with occasional hop. Voice: harsh cawing cry.

Jackdaw *Corvus monedula*: 33 cm (13″)   Resident throughout region north to central Scandinavia. Inhabits wide variety of sites from open farmland to buildings, cliffs and rocky areas. Smallest of the black crows of region with prominent **grey nape** and pale blue-grey eye. Movement in flight and on ground much quicker and more jerky than larger crows with rather bobbing walk. Very social, often mixing with ROOKS or STARLINGS (p. 208) for feeding and roosting. Nests communally in holes in trees or buildings. Voice: commonest note a typical short, harsh *'jac'*.

Chough *Pyrrhocorax pyrrhocorax*: 39 cm (15″)   Resident in western Britain and France. Inhabits mountainous and coastal cliffs and rocks. Identified by all-black plumage, **red bill and legs**. Buoyant and acrobatic in flight, often soaring with widely spread, upturned feathers at wing-tips. Occurs in small flocks or parties and in some areas nests semi-colonially. Flicks wings and tail while calling when perched. Very active on ground, hopping, walking and running. Voice: short, harsh *'chuf'* from which the bird gets its name, also has Jackdaw-like cry.

ROOK

imm

JACKDAW

imm

CHOUGH

15 cm (6 in.)

CROWS (PASSERIFORMES; CORVIDAE)

Magpie *Pica pica*: 46 cm (18") Resident throughout region except northernmost Scotland. Completely cosmopolitan in its habitat, occurring virtually everywhere and increasingly a bird of suburban areas. Highly distinctive, unmistakable bird, only **large black-and-white long-tailed** land bird of region. Flight appears weak, virtually no gliding, and long tail gives bird rather cumbersome appearance. When feeding on ground walks with tail held clear or hops sideways. Usually singly or in pairs, but will roost communally outside breeding season. Voice: loud, harsh raucous cries or chattering notes.

Nutcracker *Nucifraga caryocatactes*: 33 cm (13") Resident in southern Scandinavia and in small numbers in extreme south-east of region. In some years the population erupts westward when large numbers may appear as far west as Britain. Normally confined to coniferous forests but at times of migration may occur anywhere. **White** on **tail-tip and under tail coverts** very distinctive in flight. Very undulating flight, very JAY-like with equally rounded wings. Regularly perches on topmost twigs of trees, hopping in rather ungainly manner when feeding on ground. Singly or in pairs during breeding season, otherwise in small flocks or parties. Voice: high-pitched cawing and variety of croaking notes.

Jay *Garrulus glandarius*: 34 cm (13·5") Resident throughout region except northernmost Scandinavia. Inhabits wide variety of sites but mainly woodland areas, increasingly moving in to parks and gardens, often near town centres. Particularly fond of acorns which it collects and buries for subsequent food. **Blue-and-white wing-patches** and **prominent white rump** in flight distinguishes the species. Crown feathers can be raised to form crest. Hops actively on ground, often jerking wings. Rarely feeds in open country and usually confined to woodland where flight active amongst trees but very undulating and weak looking over any distance. Usually singly or in pairs, but roosts communally and forms small parties outside breeding season. Voice: loud, harsh screeching cry; when uttered in woodland often followed for a short while by complete silence.

Siberian Jay *Perisoreus infaustus*: 31 cm (12") Resident in central and northern Scandinavia. Inhabits woodland areas, principally coniferous, but also in some deciduous woods and outside breeding season near human habitation. Typical JAY-like shape but rather uniform plumage with strikingly contrasting **rufous colouring on wings and tail** very obvious in flight. Rather small billed but tail length proportionately greater than Jay. Shy when breeding, but confident with man at other times. Very active when feeding in trees, often moving through branches like tit (p. 164), and will settle on outermost twigs to feed on pine-cones. Voice: usually silent when breeding but rather loud nasal double note at other times.

162

MAGPIE

NUTCRACKER

JAY

SIBERIAN JAY

15 cm (6 in.)

TITS (PASSERIFORMES; PARIDAE) *Small, tame, acrobatic birds usually brightly coloured or uniform with dark cap. Form flocks of mixed species when not breeding. Sexes, winter and summer plumages similar.*

Great Tit *Parus major*: 14 cm (5·5″) Summer visitor to northern Scandinavia, resident elsewhere in region. Inhabits wide variety of sites with trees and shrubs, ranging from woodland to gardens, parks and orchards. **Largest of the familiar garden tits** with **black stripe on yellow under-parts**, regularly visiting bird-tables and frequently attacking the tops of milk bottles. Less commonly flocks than other species and less inclined to mix, usually confining to its own species. Seeks food lower in the trees or even on the ground. Voice: wide variety of calls, most familiar a Chaffinch-like '*pink*', and song said to resemble the sharpening of a saw.

Blue Tit *Parus caeruleus*: 11·5 cm (4·5″) Resident throughout region, north to central Scandinavia. Inhabits wide variety of woodland and areas of open trees and bushes, usually avoiding pure coniferous woods. Very much associated with man in towns, parks and gardens. Regularly moves to reedbeds in winter months. **Commonest tit** of region and probably the most closely associated with man. The only **small blue-and-yellow bird** of the region. Behaviour similar to GREAT TIT but more aggressive and less inclined to visit ground, feeding on branches and trunks of trees and will move up tree in manner of TREECREEPER (p. 170). More readily attacks milk bottles than Great Tits and will even enter houses to tear wallpaper or peck at putty. Voice: typical calls include a series of scolding notes often followed by a long trill.

Coal Tit *Parus ater*: 11·5 cm (4·5″) Resident throughout region north to central Scandinavia. Inhabits wide variety of sites but favours coniferous woodlands more than other species. Appears smaller and of **slighter build than other tits**, distinctly **shorter tailed**. Less confiding than GREAT TIT but will visit bird-tables in winter months. Commonly mixes with BLUE TITS and other species in winter. Feeds more commonly on trunks of trees than other tits but in conifers will search the outer branches. Voice: thin, Goldcrest-like (p. 196) call and several notes similar to Great Tit, but higher pitched.

Crested Tit *Parus cristatus*: 11·5 cm (4·5″) Resident throughout region north to central Scandinavia, except British Isles where absent apart from isolated community in central Scotland. Inhabits woodland areas, mainly conifers, but also some mixed woodland sites. Readily distinguished as **only tit** of region **with crest**. Less sociable than other tits but will join with COAL TITS in coniferous woodlands, a species it closely resembles in habits. Voice: soft trilling call and high-pitched triple note.

GREAT TIT

imm

ad

BLUE TIT

ad

imm

COAL TIT

imm

ad

CRESTED TIT

15 cm (6 in.)

TITS (PASSERIFORMES; PARIDAE)

Siberian Tit *Parus cinctus*: 13·5 cm (5·5″)   Resident through-out central and northern Scandinavia, inhabiting coniferous and birch forests. Northern replacement of MARSH TIT, differing by being browner and larger with **large throat-patch** and **dusky flanks**. Lacks neat appearance of other tits, having a rather 'scruffy' look. Voice: similar to Willow Tit but more drawn out.

Marsh Tit *Parus palustris*: 11·5 cm (4·5″)   Resident through-out region north to central Scandinavia and northern England. Absent Ireland and Scotland. Inhabits deciduous and mixed woodlands and some scrub areas. In spite of name has no attachment to marshlands. Mostly resembles WILLOW TIT, differing in having **glossy black cap** and **no pale area on wings**; generally browner and less grey than Willow Tit, tendency to have smaller black bib. Rarely more than two or three individuals in mixed winter tit flocks. More commonly feeds in lower vegetation than other tits, rarely found in tree canopy. Voice: differs from Willow Tit in being less grating, a distinctive *'pitchuo'* note.

Willow Tit *Parus montanus*: 11·5 cm (4·5″)   Resident through-out region except northernmost Scandinavia, northernmost Scotland and Ireland. Found in wide range of woodland habitat but in spite of name shows no strong preference for willows. Closely resembles MARSH TIT, differing by having **sooty black** not glossy black **cap** and **pale patch visible on closed wing**. Tends to be greyer than Marsh Tit with tendency to whiter under-parts. Generally has larger black bib than Marsh Tit. Far less active than other tits and more regularly found feeding close to the ground, often searching amongst dead leaves, etc., at base of trees. Voice: less vocal than Marsh Tit, but typical notes a very harsh *'chay'* and rather thin *'eez-eez-eez'*. Song very untit-like, resembling a warbler.

LONG-TAILED TITS (PASSERIFORMES; AEGITHALIDAE)

Long-tailed Tit *Aegithalos caudatus*: 14 cm (5·5″)   Resident throughout region north to central Scandinavia. Inhabits deciduous and mixed woodland areas with increasing tendency in recent years to move into parks and gardens. Very distinctive **black, pink and white** tit with characteristic **long tail**. Birds from northern areas of region have all-white heads. Highly acrobatic in behaviour, very restless and never motionless. Never solitary and outside breeding season always in small flocks, only occasionally mixed with other tits. Visits to bird-tables in suburban areas becoming commoner. Flight looks awkward with rapidly whirring wings and long tail. Lacks undulations of most tits. Rarely settles on ground. Voice: rather soft *'uupp'* note often difficult to hear, and thin, high-pitched, Goldcrest-like (p. 196) call.

SIBERIAN TIT

MARSH TIT

glossy cap

dull cap

WILLOW TIT

LONG-TAILED TIT

white-headed race

15 cm (6 in.)

PENDULINE TITS (PASSERIFORMES; Remizidae)

Penduline Tit *Remiz pendulinus*: 11 cm (4·5″) Resident in extreme south-east of region but tendency for westward spread in recent years. Inhabits wood and scrubland on fringes of wetland areas such as marshes and ponds. Distinctively plumaged tit with **grey head** and **black face mask**. Only other tit in similar breeding habitat is longer-tailed BEARDED TIT. Movements and flight similar to BLUE TIT (p. 164). Voice: two basic notes, typical tit-like *'tsi-tsi-tsi'* and thin Robin-like (p. 178) call.

NUTHATCHES (PASSERIFORMES; Sittidae)

Nuthatch *Sitta europaea*: 14 cm (5·5″) Resident throughout region except absent in central and northern Scandinavia, Scotland and Ireland. Inhabits wide range of woodland areas from forests to parkland and more open gardens. Only small bird of region with longish straight bill and **grey coloration** that **creeps about on tree-trunks**. Stubby appearance and very active. Searches for food on trunks and branches of trees, always moving head first either upwards or downwards, with jerky action; tail not used for support. Occasionally found on ground where progresses with series of hops. Often feeds on nuts, opening them by wedging them in cracks in trees and hammering with bill. Frequent visitor to bird-tables and regularly uses nest-boxes. Often mixes in small numbers with tit flocks in winter months. Voice: wide variety of calls, typically loud and ringing or repetitive and piping.

REEDLINGS (PASSERIFORMES; Timaliidae)

Bearded Tit *Panurus biarmicus*: 16·5 cm (6·5″) Resident in south-east England and Holland. Found exclusively in large reed-beds. The only small bird with a long tail likely to be encountered in reed-beds. Moves amongst reed stems with jerky, climbing action, though rarely sits motionless near top. Characteristic weak, whirring, undulating **flight usually low over reeds when long tail very obvious**, dropping from flight into reeds and out of sight when settling. Occurs in large parties outside breeding season, often moving to less extensive reed areas for the winter. Voice: very vocal, a ringing, metallic *'pinng'*.

PENDULINE TIT

ad

imm

NUTHATCH

15 cm (6 in.)

BEARDED TIT

♀

♂

WALLCREEPERS (PASSERIFORMES; SITTIDAE)

Wallcreeper *Tichodroma muraria*: 16·5 cm (6·5") Resident in extreme south-east of region. Inhabits buildings and rocky sites in mountainous country. Although looks like TREE-CREEPER, in fact closely related to NUTHATCH (p. 168). Distinctive. **Decurved bill** and **crimson flashes on broad rounded wings**. Wings continually flicked during food searching. Flight butterfly-like. Voice: Treecreeper-like but louder, clear and piping and rising in pitch.

TREECREEPERS (PASSERIFORMES; CERTHIIDAE)

Treecreeper *Certhia familiaris*: 12·5 cm (5") Resident in east of region north to central Scandinavia and throughout British Isles. Inhabits coniferous and mixed woodlands, particularly on upland areas. In British Isles also found in variety of sites, mixed woods, parks and gardens. **Creeps mouse-like up tree-trunks** and along branches, always moving upwards in spiral action starting from base of each tree. Stiff tail is used for support. For differences from Short-toed Treecreeper, see below. Often mixes with tit (p. 164) flocks in winter. Voice: very high pitched; song, a series of notes and rather prolonged single call *'tseee'*.

Short-toed Treecreeper *Certhia brachydactyla*: 12·5 cm (5") Resident throughout region except British Isles and Scandinavia. Inhabits woodland sites ranging from parks and gardens to areas of scattered trees. Virtually indistinguishable from TREECREEPER, but possible distinctions are call, distribution and brownish flanks of this species. Voice: louder, less high pitched than Treecreeper and single harsh *'skree'* note.

WRENS (PASSERIFORMES; TROGLODYTIDAE)

Wren *Troglodytes troglodytes*: 9·5 cm (3·75") Resident throughout region north to central Scandinavia. Inhabits wide variety of sites, most familiar in woodland and scrub but also in open sites, gardens, parks, cliffs and moors. Common in suburban gardens. Familiar and distinctive small bird with **warm brown plumage** and **cocked tail**. Very active, usually on or near ground foraging amongst litter. Flight like whirring bee, always direct and close to ground. Voice: very loud warbling song and prolonged churring when alarmed.

DIPPERS (PASSERIFORMES; CINCLIDAE)

Dipper *Cinclus cinclus*: 18 cm (7") Resident in suitable habitat throughout region. Inhabits fast-flowing upland streams with some wanderings in winter months. Distinctive, rather fat-bodied, short-tailed bird, examples from northern Europe lacking chestnut on under-parts. **Constantly 'bobs' body** when perched with downward jerk of tail. **Swims and dives with ease** and will 'walk' on stream bed. Never seen far from water. Voice: metallic clicking notes and Wren-like song.

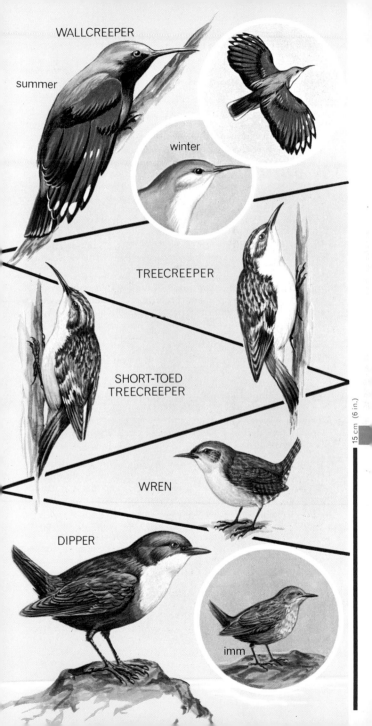

WALLCREEPER

summer

winter

TREECREEPER

SHORT-TOED
TREECREEPER

WREN

DIPPER

imm

15 cm (6 in.)

THRUSHES (PASSERIFORMES; TURDIDAE) *Medium-sized song-birds mainly feeding on ground where they hop, but equally at home in trees or bushes. Slender bill. Communal outside breeding season. Females similar or browner than males, immatures speckled; winter and summer plumages similar.*

Mistle Thrush *Turdus viscivorus*: 27 cm (10·5") Resident throughout region, north to southern Scandinavia. Summer visitor to central Scandinavia, absent northern Scandinavia. Inhabits wide variety of sites, favouring deciduous or mixed woodland, but also occurring in open parkland, suburban gardens, etc. Larger and greyer than SONG THRUSH with more **upright stance**, **black**, **round spots** and white tips to outer tail feathers. White under-wing flashes noticeable in flight which is very woodpecker-like (p. 148) with strong undulations. Generally shy, but very aggressive when nesting. Voice: song loud, Blackbird-like (p. 174), usually delivered from very prominent perch, even in extremely severe weather. Flight call harsh and grating.

Song Thrush *Turdus philomelos*: 23 cm (9") Summer visitor to extreme east of region and Scandinavia, resident elsewhere and extreme south of Scandinavia. Inhabits almost all woodland areas, particularly favouring deciduous sites, parks, orchards, gardens, etc. Generally the commonest speckled thrush of region, smaller and browner than MISTLE THRUSH with less upright stance and markedly **buff under-wing** (not rich colouring of REDWING). Flight lacks periods of wing closure as in Mistle Thrush, usually very direct. When feeding on ground hops and runs **often stopping with head cocked on one side**. Regularly breaks snail shells against stones when feeding. Voice: song loud and clear, each note or phrase usually repeated at least twice. Flight call a thin '*seep*', very Redwing-like.

Redwing *Turdus iliacus*: 21 cm (8·25") Summer visitor to central and northern Scandinavia, winter visitor throughout remainder of region; small numbers now breeding in northern Scotland. Inhabits northern forests and areas of scattered trees. During winter more regularly found in open country, favouring farmland. Smallest of the common thrushes, darker than SONG THRUSH with **prominent pale stripe over eye** and **chestnut flanks** and under-wing. Behaviour similar to Song Thrush, very gregarious in winter, particularly favouring berry hedges, often in large communal winter groups mixed with other thrushes. Voice: song shorter, less varied than Song Thrush, flight note a thin '*seeep*'.

MISTLE THRUSH

SONG THRUSH

REDWING

15 cm (6 in.)

THRUSHES (PASSERIFORMES; TURDIDAE)

Fieldfare *Turdus pilaris*: 25·5 cm (10″) Summer visitor to central and northern Scandinavia, resident southern Scandinavia and extreme east of region, winter visitor elsewhere. Inhabits wide range of open woodland, parks, gardens, etc., occurring more regularly on farmland in winter months. Distinctively plumaged thrush having strong contrast with **grey head and rump, chestnut back** and **dark tail**. The grey head can give a rather pigeon-like appearance when viewed across some distance of open ground. Flight and behaviour most closely resembles MISTLE THRUSH (p. 172). Very gregarious and rather shy in winter, often mixed with REDWINGS (p. 172). Voice: twittering song and loud, chuckling flight note *'cha-cha-chack'*.

Ring Ousel *Turdus torquatus*: 24 cm (9·5″) Summer visitor to British Isles and Scandinavia. Inhabits upland areas of moorland and mountain, occasionally with a few scattered trees. Differs from BLACKBIRD in having **white gorget, pale wing-patch** and scaly, rather grey appearance. Flight wilder, more erratic. Behaviour similar to Blackbird in many respects but is much shyer and more readily perches in exposed positions. Aggressive when nesting. Often mixed with other thrushes on migration. Voice: song rather simple, consisting of few notes, a piping call note and harsh, chattering alarm call.

Blackbird *Turdus merula*: 25 cm (10″) Summer visitor to central Scandinavia, absent northern Scandinavia, resident throughout remainder of region. Very cosmopolitan, habitats ranging from mixed woodland and open country to parks, orchards and town gardens. Perhaps the commonest and one of the most familiar birds of the region. Flight is often accompanied by distinctive flicking action of wings, tail raised upwards when settling, then slowly lowered. Hops rather jauntily when feeding, cocking head on one side while standing motionless. Tends to skulk more than other thrushes, rarely far from cover and less likely to be encountered in very open situations. Voice: loud, persistent ticking note used regularly before roosting, fluty song lacks repetition of Song Thrush.

FIELDFARE

RING OUSEL

♂

♀

BLACKBIRD

♂

♀

15 cm (6 in.)

CHATS and STARTS (PASSERIFORMES; TURDIDAE) *Small Robin-like thrushes, many brightly coloured; perch very upright, many species in very exposed positions. Wheatears have white rumps, chats white flashes in wing or/and tail; starts and nightingales have red tails, in some species males more brightly coloured than females. Immatures resemble females. Summer and winter plumages usually similar.*

Wheatear *Oenanthe oenanthe*: 15 cm (6″) Summer visitor throughout region. Inhabits open areas of moors, downs and uplands. Immediately distinguished by conspicuous **white rump** and **black-and-white tail pattern**, very active, moving with series of long hops or short flights. Usually seen on ground or very exposed perch. Much bobbing and flitting, often chasing flies, frequently hovering on breeding ground. Voice: squeaky warbling song and harsh chacking call note.

Stonechat *Saxicola torquata*: 12·5 cm (5″) Summer visitor to south and east of region, resident in northern France and British Isles. Inhabits areas of heath, moorland and open scrub, particularly coastal during winter. Very **round-headed short-tailed bird**, perching in very exposed positions on fences and bushes, particularly favouring gorse. Continually spreads and flicks its tail with regular flicking wing action. Usually seen in pairs throughout the year. Flies for only short distances, usually keeping low with very jerky action. Voice: song a squeaking warbling, often given in flight; harsh chacking call note resembling stones being knocked together.

Whinchat *Saxicola rubetra*: 12·5 cm (5″) Summer visitor throughout region except southern Ireland and northernmost Scandinavia. Habitat similar to STONECHAT but slightly more associated with grassland and water. Slimmer and less upright than Stonechat but similarly short-tailed. Distinguished by **pale stripe over eye** and **white patches in tail**. Behaviour similar to Stonechat but more readily perches in trees, always in exposed positions, usually very active at dusk. Voice: very similar to Stonechat but call note less harsh, more musical.

WHEATEAR

STONECHAT

WHINCHAT

15 cm (6 in.)

CHATS and STARTS (PASSERIFORMES; Turdidae)

Redstart *Phoenicurus phoenicurus*: 14 cm (5·5") Summer visitor throughout region except Ireland. Inhabits mixed woodland, parks, gardens, etc., and open areas usually with stone walls or ruined buildings. Behaviour rather Robin-like (see below) but much more confined to foliage where very active. Rarely seen on ground. Makes regular fly-catching sallies and perches with strange but **distinctive tail-shivering movement**. Voice: call note very Willow Warbler-like, a single *'whooet'*. Song rather brief, jangling and Robin-like.

Black Redstart *Phoenicurus ochruros*: 14 cm (5·5") Resident in southern England and western France, summer visitor elsewhere in region north to southern Scandinavia. Inhabits more open areas than REDSTART favouring cliffs, mountainous areas, buildings and town centres. Adult males distinctive, females and immatures differ from Redstart in having sooty grey, less brown plumage particularly on **under-parts** where **total lack of buff**. Tail less brightly rufous. Behaviour, stance and movements closely resemble Redstart but more regularly seen on ground and usually perched in very exposed positions rather than seeking cover. Voice: song Redstart-like but including a distinctive grating or grinding noise. Frequently used, single *'tic'* call note.

Robin *Erithacus rubecula*: 14 cm (5·5") Resident throughout region except Scandinavia where summer visitor except far north. Inhabits wide variety of sites from woodland and forest to gardens and scrub, a common bird of town parks and suburbia, particularly in west of region. Probably the most familiar and easiest bird to identify in region. Often very tame and approachable near human habitations but elsewhere rather shy and retiring. Stands very upright, appearing plump, round and neckless. Regularly feeds on ground and often attracted to bird-tables. Very aggressive in defence of territory. Voice: song consists of short, warbling phrases, call note a regularly used *'tic'*.

REDSTART

autumn ♂

♀

♂

autumn ♂

BLACK REDSTART

♂

♀

ROBIN

imm

ad

15 cm (6 in.)

CHATS and STARTS (PASSERIFORMES; Turdidae)

Nightingale *Luscinia megarhynchos*: 16·5 cm (6·5″) Summer visitor throughout region except Scandinavia, Scotland and Ireland. Inhabits deciduous woodland, thickets and areas of dense shrubs. More frequently heard than seen, very shy and retiring and invariably solitary. Shape and movements similar to large Robin with **long reddish tail** which is frequently held in a cocked position. Differs from THRUSH NIGHTINGALE in range, browner, richer coloration of upper-parts and brighter tail. Voice: song extremely varied and famous for its richness and quality, usually delivered from dense cover. Sings regularly in daytime but continues after nightfall when most other species have ceased.

Thrush Nightingale *Luscinia luscinia*: 16·5 cm (6·5″) Summer visitor to southern Scandinavia. Inhabits similar areas to NIGHTINGALE but usually favours damper sites. General appearance and behaviour as Nightingale; differs from Nightingale in limited range in region, in having greyer, less brown upper-parts, and darker, less reddish rufous tail. **Breast** usually more **mottled with grey** than Nightingale. Voice: very similar to Nightingale, perhaps slightly higher pitched and with larger numbers of harsh notes.

Bluethroat *Luscinia svecica*: 14 cm (5·5″) Summer visitor to east of region and throughout Scandinavia. Inhabits low-growing scrub areas and thickets, usually closely associated with damp sites. Rather shy, REDSTART-like (p. 178), distinguished by **distinctive head and breast markings** and characteristic tail pattern. Red-spotted race found in Scandinavia, white-spotted race in east of region. Active, frequently on ground. Tail spread and flicked almost continually, and body often bobbed in Robin-like manner. Flight usually over short distances and close to ground, and diving rapidly back into cover. Voice: call note a persistent *'tac'*; song varied and musical and often given in flight, and may include mimicked phrases of other species.

NIGHTINGALE

THRUSH NIGHTINGALE

BLUETHROAT

♀

winter

summer

red-spotted race

♂

imm

summer

white-spotted race

♂

15 cm (6 in.)

WARBLERS (PASSERIFORMES; SYLVIIDAE) *Small, generally migratory, insect-eating birds, very active. Many species difficult to observe. Song very helpful for identification. Plumages usually similar irrespective of sex, age or season. Can be conveniently divided into five groups.*

Locustella warblers   Very shy and retiring, confining themselves to dense cover, often in damp areas, tail rather heavy and distinctly rounded.

Grasshopper Warbler *Locustella naevia*: 13 cm (5″)   Summer visitor throughout region north to southern Scandinavia. Inhabits heaths and scrubland, often favouring marshes but equally at home in dry areas. General appearance very slim and tapered. Very secretive. Reluctant to fly, moving easily amongst dense, tangled vegetation. Regularly **bobs and cocks tail**. Voice: song distinctive, always uttered from dense vegetation, said to resemble a fisherman's reel. Very high pitched and carries for long distances; movement of the bird's head appearing to alter the location of the singing bird.

Savi's Warbler *Locustella luscinioides*: 14 cm (5·5″)   Summer visitor to south-east England, France, Low Countries and Northern Germany. Inhabits marshes with dense vegetation, particularly favouring reed-beds. Larger, more uniform version of GRASSHOPPER WARBLER with **brown upper-parts**. Less skulking, more regularly seen perched in exposed positions such as reed-heads when **white chin** apparent. Voice: song similar to Grasshopper Warbler but slower, louder and lower pitched, usually delivered from exposed perch.

Acrocephalus warblers   Difficult group to observe, confined to wet areas, generally brown with rounded tails and flattened foreheads. Often skulking with churring, repetitive songs.

Sedge Warbler *Acrocephalus schoenobaenus*: 13 cm (5″)   Summer visitor throughout region. Inhabits wide variety of scrub, hedgerows and tangled vegetation near water. **Broad pale stripe over eye**, unstreaked rufous rump and streaked upper-parts. Rarely seen in open but often on or close to ground amongst vegetation. Flight direct and low with tail spread or depressed. Voice: song often delivered in fluttering song-flight, a wide variety of harsh churring and chattering notes and often including snatches copied from other species.

Aquatic Warbler *Acrocephalus paludicola*: 13 cm (5″)   Summer visitor to northern France, Low Countries and northern Germany. Inhabits areas associated with fresh water, particularly reeds and sedges. Compared with SEDGE WARBLER distinctly yellowish with **broad, pale stripe down centre of crown** and **well-streaked rump** (note that immature Sedge Warblers can show ill-defined pale stripe on crown). More skulking than Sedge Warbler, occasionally on ground amongst vegetation and rarely flies any distance if flushed. Voice: song resembles Sedge Warbler but perhaps less varied.

GRASSHOPPER
WARBLER

SAVI'S WARBLER

SEDGE WARBLER

crown pattern

AQUATIC WARBLER

15 cm (6 in.)

WARBLERS (PASSERIFORMES; SYLVIIDAE)

Acrocephalus warblers

Great Reed Warbler *Acrocephalus arundinaceus*: 19 cm (7·5") Summer visitor to region north to English Channel and southern Scandinavia. Inhabits extensive reed-beds and vegetation fringing fresh water. Largest warbler of region approaching thrush in size but shape and behaviour typical of REED WARBLER. Stout bill lacks fineness usually associated with warblers. Less skulking than others of group, readily perching in exposed positions such as tops of bushes or overhead wires. Flight usually low over reeds with tail spread and drops very heavily back into cover. When perched **sits with tail depressed and rump pushed out** giving characteristic outline. Voice: song resembles cross between frog and Song Thrush (p. 172), often delivered from exposed perch.

Reed Warbler *Acrocephalus scirpaceus*: 12·5 cm (5") Summer visitor throughout region except northern Scandinavia, Scotland and Ireland. Inhabits any wet areas with associated reeds although increasing tendency to occur in wet but reedless sites. Rather featureless bird and extremely difficult to distinguish from MARSH WARBLER (see below) but generally richer **reddish-brown upper-parts** especially on rump and with **dark legs**. Rounded tail is carried downwards and spread during low, direct flight. Moves amongst reed stems by hopping or jerking upwards. Concentrations in reed-beds make the species appear colonial. Voice: song harsh and churring, but unlike Sedge Warbler very repetitive in character.

Marsh Warbler *Acrocephalus palustris*: 12·5 cm (5") Summer visitor to southern England and eastern France, east to southern Scandinavia. Inhabits wet area sites but not confined to reed-beds, preferring dense scrub or bushy vegetation. Very closely resembles REED WARBLER, differing in song, more **greenish or greyish coloration** of upper-parts which are uniform with rump and generally **pale legs**. Perhaps slightly plumper than Reed Warbler and more inclined to use exposed perches. Voice: more varied and musical than Reed Warbler, regularly including mimicry of a variety of other species.

Cetti's Warbler *Cettia cetti*: 14 cm (5·5") Resident in France, Belgium and southern England. Inhabits areas of dense vegetation, always associated with fresh water or marshes. Very skulking and on brief glimpses can look very WREN-like (p. 170) with **rounded tail** and **warm brown upper-parts**. Tail occasionally held in cocked position. Rarely flies any distance, keeping close to the ground. Appears to have ability of changing its position without having been seen to move. Voice: very distinctive song, loud and explosive, always given in abrupt bursts, said to resemble its name '*seet-tee*'.

GREAT REED WARBLER

REED WARBLER

MARSH WARBLER

CETTI'S WARBLER

15 cm (6 in.)

WARBLERS (PASSERIFORMES; Sylviidae)

Hippolais warblers   Uniform yellowish and greenish warblers with rather *Acrocephalus*-like (p. 182) head shape but broader bill; square tail. Rarely found near water.

Melodious Warbler *Hippolais polyglotta*: 13 cm (5″)   Summer visitor to France. Inhabits deciduous woodland, parkland, orchards, etc. Differs from ICTERINE WARBLER in having shorter, more rounded wings, noticeably **pale base to lower mandible** and **lack of pale wing panel**. Always shows **very yellow on under-parts**. Habits and actions resemble Icterine Warbler. Voice: call note rather sparrow-like; song liquid and musical, far less *Acrocephalus*-like than Icterine Warbler.

Icterine Warbler *Hippolais icterina*: 13·5 cm (5·25″)   Summer visitor to east of region and southern Scandinavia. Inhabits similar areas to MELODIOUS WARBLER and is eastern replacement of that species. Differs from Melodious Warbler in having longer, more **pointed wings** (tip of wing reaches beyond tail coverts), greener, less brown upper-parts and many individuals show **pale panel on closed wing**. Occasional very grey individuals occur which lack yellow on under-parts and with greatly reduced amounts of green in upper-parts. Active, but movements rather heavy, tending to 'crash' through vegetation. Crown feathers can be raised when alarmed to give big-headed effect. Most frequently found amongst foliage usually rather high in the tree. Voice: song loud and rather harsh recalling *Acrocephalus* warbler.

Sylvia warblers   Skulking, rather long-tailed warblers of scrub vegetation, generally more brightly coloured than other warblers, males usually more distinctive than females.

Barred Warbler *Sylvia nisoria*: 15 cm (6″)   Summer visitor to eastern Germany and southernmost Scandinavia. Inhabits thickets and bushy scrubland or edges of woodland. One of the largest *Sylvia* warblers appearing **very stout and grey** with rather stubby bill. General appearance like a rather heavy long-tailed GARDEN WARBLER (p. 188) with white-tipped tail feathers. Very skulking in behaviour with constantly flicking tail. Heavy flight is somewhat reminiscent of WRYNECK (p. 152). Voice: loud harsh call note incorporated in short, rather bursting song.

Dartford Warbler *Sylvia undata*: 12·5 cm (5″)   Resident in west of region north to southern England. Inhabits dense scrubland favouring areas of heath with gorse and heather. The only truly resident *Sylvia* warbler of region. Very long, **frequently cocked tail** is distinctive. Rather shy, usually only sitting in exposed positions when singing. Flight low and jerky over vegetation, dropping into cover when long tail obvious. Small flocks form in autumn and winter. Voice: song Whitethroat-like (p. 190), often delivered during fluttering display flight or on top of bush. Churring alarm note.

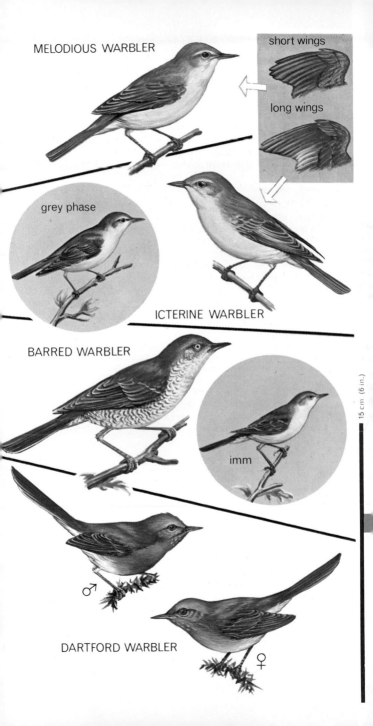

MELODIOUS WARBLER

short wings

long wings

grey phase

ICTERINE WARBLER

BARRED WARBLER

imm

15 cm (6 in.)

♂

DARTFORD WARBLER

♀

WARBLERS (PASSERIFORMES; SYLVIIDAE)

Sylvia warblers

Blackcap *Sylvia atricapilla*: 14 cm (5·5″) Summer visitor throughout region, small numbers wintering in southern England and western France. Inhabits open woodlands, parks, gardens, etc. Both sexes distinguished by **capped appearance not extending below eye**. Immatures resemble female. Less skulking than GARDEN WARBLER, often found in very exposed positions. Very active, but rarely seen on ground and moves from cover to cover with short, jerky flight. Does not appear particularly long tailed. Voice: song similar to Garden Warbler but higher pitched and with shorter phrases.

Orphean Warbler *Sylvia hortensis*: 15 cm (6″) Summer visitor to southern France. Inhabits areas of open scrub and parkland. Larger and stockier than BLACKCAP with **capped appearance extending below the white eye**, and with prominent **white outer tail feathers**. Only infrequently seen in low vegetation, preferring the foliage of higher trees. Crown feathers can be raised to give the head a peaked appearance. Voice: song of rather thrush-like warblings and a loud rasping call note.

Garden Warbler *Sylvia borin*: 14 cm (5·5″) Summer visitor throughout region. Inhabits open mixed woodland, parks and large gardens. Very uniform in appearance, **lacking any distinctive plumage characters**. Rather short, stoutish bill and bluish-grey legs help with identification. Often shows pale marks on bend of wing. Rather skulking, otherwise shape and behaviour similar to BLACKCAP. Voice: song usually delivered from hidden position, a pleasant warbling of rather long phrases, usually quieter than similar song of Blackcap.

BLACKCAP

♂

♀

ORPHEAN WARBLER

♂

♀

GARDEN WARBLER

15 cm (6 in.)

WARBLERS (PASSERIFORMES; SYLVIIDAE)

Sylvia warblers

Whitethroat *Sylvia communis*: 14 cm (5·5″)   Summer visitor throughout region north to central Scandinavia. Inhabits areas of thorn bushes, thickets and scrub, usually with low, dense vegetation. Very active, but rather skulking, darting in and out of cover, often cocks tail and raises crown feathers to form rather poorly defined crest. Browner than LESSER WHITETHROAT with slightly longer tail and **prominent rufous fringes to wing feathers**. Flight is rather jerky but direct, almost always low to ground and ends with bird diving into cover. Voice: rather harsh, brief, but fast song delivered from exposed perch or in fluttering song flight. Harsh churring notes when alarmed.

Lesser Whitethroat *Sylvia curruca*: 13·5 cm (5·25″)   Summer visitor throughout region except northern and western Britain, northern Scandinavia and western France. Inhabits areas of low woodland, parks and scrub. Greyer and whiter than WHITETHROAT lacking rufous on wings and with distinct **dark area behind eye forming mask**. Shorter tailed than Whitethroat with dark legs. As skulking as Whitethroat but less inclined to keep to ground cover, equally at home in tree foliage. Flight and movements similar to Whitethroat. Voice: unwarbler-like rattling song similar to opening phrases of Yellowhammer (p. 220), rarely delivered from an exposed perch. Lacks song flight.

Subalpine Warbler *Sylvia cantillans*: 12 cm (4·75″)   Rather scarce visitor to extreme south of region. Inhabits areas of open scrub and thickets. Somewhat resembles a smaller, paler DARTFORD WARBLER (p. 186) with short tail and **white moustachial stripes**. Rather skulking but has characteristic flicking and tail-spreading movements while moving through cover. Behaviour much like Dartford Warbler with flight and movements similar to WHITETHROAT. Voice: song musical, rather Whitethroat-like but lacking any harsh notes, delivered in fluttering song flight. Chattering alarm note.

WHITETHROAT

♂

♀

LESSER
WHITETHROAT

SUBALPINE WARBLER

♂

♀

15 cm (6 in.)

WARBLERS (PASSERIFORMES; SYLVIIDAE)

Phylloscopus warblers Difficult to identify, small yellowish-green warblers, generally not skulking, inhabiting outer foliage of trees and bushes. Most readily identified by song.

Willow Warbler *Phylloscopus trochilus*: 11 cm (4·25″) Summer visitor throughout region, inhabiting wide variety of sites from mixed woodlands, open parklands, bushes, etc. Probably the commonest warbler of region, very similar to CHIFFCHAFF and probably only safely distinguished when familiarity with the two species is achieved. Compared with Chiffchaff is longer winged with rather slimmer appearance and usually yellower below and greener above. **Leg colour** varies but is usually **pale**. Less inclined to flick wings and tail than Chiffchaff. Flight is jerky and fluttering, often hovering amongst upper foliage picking food from leaves. Occasionally makes fly-catching sallies from cover. Will also feed on or near the ground but less likely to do so than Chiffchaff. Voice: **song** consists of a **musical series of descending notes**. Call note, a quiet '*hoo-eet*' tending to be disyllabic.

Chiffchaff *Phylloscopus collybita*: 11 cm (4·25″) Summer visitor throughout region except northernmost Scotland and northernmost Scandinavia. Small numbers winter in south-west Britain and western France. Inhabits similar areas to WILLOW WARBLER but usually favouring sites with taller trees and less ground cover. General appearance similar to Willow Warbler but tends to be more active with almost continual movements of wings and tail. Shorter winged than Willow Warbler, bird appearing stubbier. Tends to appear browner above and less clear yellow below. Birds from Scandinavia are distinctly greyer above and whiter below. **Legs always dark**. Habits similar to Willow Warbler. Voice: **monotonous repetitive song**, likened to the bird's name '*chiff-chaff-chiff-chaff*'. Call note a monosyllabic '*weet*'.

Wood Warbler *Phylloscopus sibilatrix*: 12·5 cm (5″) Summer visitor throughout region except central and northern Scandinavia and Ireland. Inhabits open mixed and deciduous woodland. Largest of the *Phylloscopus* warblers with striking **yellow breast sharply demarked from clear white belly**, intense yellow edgings to feathers of wings and tail. Wings appear very long and are often drooped when perched. Very active but lacks wing- and tail-flicking. Generally confined to trees, rarely on or near ground. Voice: trilling song rather reminiscent of spinning coin on a tin plate, sometimes delivered in song flight.

WILLOW WARBLER

imm

15 cm (6 in.)

CHIFFCHAFF

WOOD WARBLER

WARBLERS (PASSERIFORMES; SYLVIIDAE)

Phylloscopus warblers

Greenish Warbler *Phylloscopus trochiloides*: 11 cm (4·25") Summer visitor to eastern Scandinavia. Inhabits open mixed woodlands and edges of dense cover. Similar to CHIFFCHAFF (p. 192) but differs in having more prominent pale stripe over eye and less yellow under-parts. **Single pale wing-bar** is straight and formed by whitish spots on tips of wing coverts. **Legs dark**. Smaller, less brown than similar ARCTIC WARBLER with distinctive greyish-green colour to mantle. Very active but usually secretive, keeping well amongst cover high in trees. Will flick wings and tail occasionally. Voice: song is high pitched, short and loud consisting of warbling and trilling.

Bonelli's Warbler *Phylloscopus bonelli*: 11·5 cm (4·5") Summer visitor to western and southern France and southern Germany. Inhabits woodland sites mainly in upland areas. Rather pale warbler, lacking green and yellow on body plumage but with brightly edged wing and tail feathers and with **prominent yellow rump** although this is often hidden by closed wings. Very active but inconspicuous, mainly in tree foliage where feeds like WILLOW WARBLER (p. 192). Voice: call note similar to Willow Warbler. Short song is similar to start of Wood Warbler's trill (p. 192).

Arctic Warbler *Phylloscopus borealis*: 12 cm (4·75") Summer visitor to northern Scandinavia. Inhabits areas of scrubland and forest in arctic zone. Distinctly larger than WILLOW WARBLER (p. 192) with broad, straight and **long pale stripe over eye** and **two pale wing-bars although one is often inconspicuous** or absent. **Legs pale**. Much browner than smaller GREENISH WARBLER. Habits typical of *Phylloscopus* warblers, usually confined to outer foliage of trees but also on or near the ground. Voice: rather rattling, monotonous song and a variety of clicking notes all somewhat metallic.

GREENISH WARBLER

BONELLI'S WARBLER

ARCTIC WARBLER

15 cm (6 in.)

WARBLERS (PASSERIFORMES; SYLVIIDAE)

Phylloscopus warblers

Yellow-browed Warbler *Phylloscopus inornatus*: 10 cm (4″) Scarce, annual migrant from Asia. Smallest *Phylloscopus* warbler, resembling crest in general appearance but longer tailed and lacking crown markings. Greenish yellow above and whitish below. Habits similar to WILLOW WARBLER (p. 192), indulging in fly-catching sallies and frequent flicking of wings and tail. Distinguished from immature GOLDCREST by longer tail and **long, prominent, yellowish stripe over eye**. Voice: Willow Warbler-like *'hooeet'*.

CRESTS (PASSERIFORMES; REGULIDAE) *Smallest birds of region, rather warbler-like (p. 182) but short tailed and more agile with striking head pattern. Distinct preference for conifers. Often very tame and confiding. Sexes, winter and summer plumages similar. Immatures lack strong head markings.*

Goldcrest *Regulus regulus*: 9 cm (3·5″) Resident throughout region except northernmost Scandinavia. Inhabits woodland areas especially coniferous sites although sometimes well away from conifers in winter months. Small size distinctive. Differs from FIRECREST in lack of broad white stripe over eye and no bronze shoulder coloration. Orange crown of male usually hidden by yellow feathering. Immatures differ from *Phylloscopus* warblers (p. 192) by lack of pale stripe over eye. Very active and acrobatic while moving through foliage, often joining tit flocks in winter. Flight weak and fluttering with fast wing-beats. Voice: thin *'zi-zi-zi'* call note similar to Treecreeper (p. 170), song equally thin and piping.

Firecrest *Regulus ignicapillus*: 9 cm (3·5″) Summer visitor in east of region north to northern Germany, resident or winter visitor in west of region north to southern England. Inhabits similar areas to GOLDCREST but shows less preference for conifers. Similar to Goldcrest, differing in higher-pitched voice, **black stripe through eye**, **broad white stripe over eye** and bronze patch on shoulders. Green of upper-parts more intense. Voice: similar to Goldcrest but deeper tone and shorter song, with regularly used single note.

DUNNOCKS (PASSERIFORMES; PRUNELLIDAE)

Dunnock *Prunella modularis*: 14·5 cm (5·75″) Resident throughout region except central and northern Scandinavia where summer visitor. Inhabits almost any areas with bush or scrub cover, from woodland to suburban gardens. Predominantly ground living, moving with **shuffling gait**. Inconspicuous rather than retiring. **Regularly flicks wings**, sometimes independently of each other. Solitary. Voice: regularly used, thin, high-pitched note; song a warble resembling cross between Robin and Wren but lacking strength of latter and usually delivered from exposed perch.

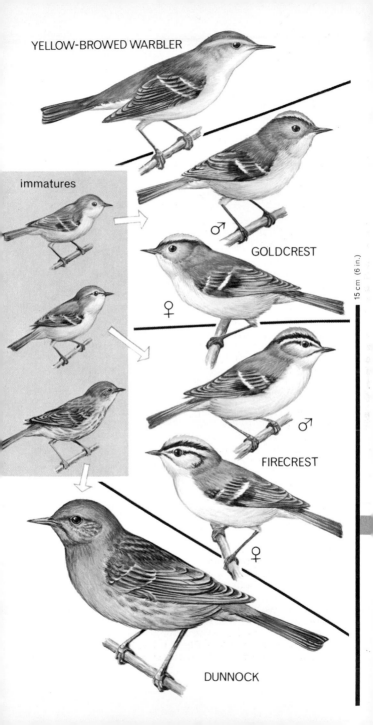

YELLOW-BROWED WARBLER

immatures

♂

GOLDCREST

♀

♂

FIRECREST

♀

DUNNOCK

15 cm (6 in.)

FLYCATCHERS (PASSERIFORMES; MUSCICAPIDAE) *Rather small, upright, perching birds, feeding in typical manner of sallying forth from perch, catching fly in flight and returning to perch. Males with more contrasting plumage than females (except Spotted Flycatcher). Immatures and males in winter resemble females.*

Spotted Flycatcher *Muscicapa striata*: 14 cm (5·5″) Summer visitor throughout region. Inhabits areas of open woodlands, parks, gardens, etc. Feeds from more exposed perches than other flycatchers, with rather neckless appearance and **regular flicking of wings and tail**. Usually solitary. Flight is very erratic when feeding with frequent changes in direction and manoeuvres when chasing flies. Rarely alights on ground or tops of trees, preferring fences and exposed lower branches. Voice: song a short series of unmusical squeaky notes; call note a thin, shrill '*zeee*'.

Pied Flycatcher *Ficedula hypoleuca*: 13 cm (5″) Summer visitor throughout region except south-east England, Ireland and western France. Inhabits variety of woodland sites. Smaller and plumper than SPOTTED FLYCATCHER. Strikingly **black-and-white male** differs from similar COLLARED FLYCATCHER in having **dark rump**, less white on wings and forehead and no white collar. Females and immatures very similar to Collared Flycatcher (see below) but tend to be browner. Often alights on ground and when fly-catching rarely returns to same perch. Tail continually cocked and flicked. Will nest readily in tit-style nest-boxes (Spotted Flycatchers preferring open-fronted Robin-style boxes). Voice: single metallic call note; song rather unmusical and repetitive, occasionally including a trill.

Collared Flycatcher *Ficedula albicollis*: 12·5 cm (5″) Summer visitor to eastern France and southern Germany. Inhabits similar areas to PIED FLYCATCHER. Closely resembles Pied Flycatcher. Males differ in having broad **white collar on nape**, **white rump** and more extensive white on wings and forehead. Females and immatures more difficult to distinguish but generally greyer with tendency to pale rump and more extensive white on wings. Habits as Pied Flycatcher but less inclined to settle on ground and slightly more secretive. Voice: song similar to Pied Flycatcher but softer; call note loud and disyllabic, less metallic than Pied Flycatcher.

Red-breasted Flycatcher *Ficedula parva*: 11·5 cm (4·5″) Summer visitor to extreme east of region. Inhabits deciduous woodlands. Smallest flycatcher of region and can vary greatly in feeding behaviour; sometimes sits in very exposed areas as typical flycatcher, at other times very secretive, moving through cover in manner of a warbler. Frequent tail-flicking and wing-drooping show characteristic **white flashes on sides of tail**. Voice: most regularly used note a short sharp '*tic*'; song a series of rather short but varied warblings.

SPOTTED FLYCATCHER

imm

ad

winter
♂

PIED FLYCATCHER

♂

♀

♀

COLLARED FLYCATCHER

♂

♀

♂

RED-BREASTED FLYCATCHER

15 cm (6 in.)

PIPITS (PASSERIFORMES; MOTACILLIDAE) *Generally brown, streaked, ground-living, wagtail-like (p. 204) birds; much slimmer, longer and finer built than larks (p. 154). Sexes, winter and summer plumages similar.*

Tawny Pipit *Anthus campestris*: 16·5 cm (6·5″) Summer visitor in region north to English Channel and southern Scandinavia. Inhabits generally dry open areas of sand and heath. Largest and palest of the breeding pipits of the region, also the most **wagtail-like** (p. 204). Very **long legged** and rather longer tailed than other pipits. Moves very rapidly on ground, occasionally moving tail in manner of wagtail. Flight very wagtail-like with marked undulations although bird's appearance in air is slightly heavier and bulkier than wagtail. Voice: song simple and repetitive, delivered in display flight after which bird drops to ground; call notes similar to Yellow Wagtail (p. 204) or Tree Sparrow (p.226).

Meadow Pipit *Anthus pratensis*: 14·5 cm (5·75″) Summer visitor to much of Scandinavia, resident in extreme south of Scandinavia and throughout remainder of region. Inhabits wide range of open country, heath, moors, farmland, etc. More regularly in wet areas during winter months. Commonest pipit of region. Flocks outside breeding season, often in loose groups of a few hundred birds. Differs from similar TREE PIPIT in choice of habitat, **song flight from ground**, **darkish legs** and tendency to yellowish on under-parts, not buff. Voice: song a succession of rather weak notes ending with a trill given in fluttering song flight, bird rising from ground and 'parachuting' back to ground at end of song; call note a repeated '*sipp*'.

Tree Pipit *Anthus trivialis*: 15 cm (6″) Summer visitor throughout region except Ireland. Inhabits open woodland and areas of scattered trees. Similar to MEADOW PIPIT but slightly larger and of heavier build; differs in habitat, **pale legs**, rich buff on under-parts and **song flight starting and ending from tree or exposed bush**. Less active than Meadow Pipit, walking with steady gait rather than jerky, slightly bobbing appearance of Meadow Pipit. Voice: call note very distinctive, a harsh, drawn-out '*tzeee*'. Song more musical than Meadow Pipit, sometimes given from a perch.

TAWNY PIPIT

ad

imm

song flight

MEADOW PIPIT

song flight

TREE PIPIT

15 cm (6 in.)

PIPITS (PASSERIFORMES; MOTACILLIDAE)

Red-throated Pipit *Anthus cervinus*: 14·5 cm (5·75") Summer visitor to northern Scandinavia. Inhabits open coastal and tundra areas. Rather darkish pipit lacking greenish coloration with **strongly streaked rump** and under-parts. In summer plumage the amount of russet on throat and breast is variable in extent and intensity of colour. Habits closely resemble TREE PIPIT (p. 200). Voice: song Meadow Pipit-like; calls include a sparrow-like 'churp' and a nasal disyllabic Tree Pipit-like call.

Rock/Water Pipit *Anthus spinoletta*: 16·5 cm (6·5") A variable pipit occurring in region in two distinct races. Larger and appearing longer than MEADOW or TREE PIPIT (p. 200) with **dark legs**. Voice: both races sound similar. Meadow Pipit-like song delivered in song flight, bird rising from stony promontory and 'parachuting' to ground at end of song. Call note distinctive, a single sharp call deeper than Meadow Pipit.

Rock Pipit: coastal bird occurring as summer visitor to central and northern Scandinavia, resident in southern Scandinavia, British Isles and north-west France and winter visitor to remaining coastal localities. Greyer than Meadow or Tree Pipit although birds from Scandinavia have distinctly brownish hue. **Grey** (not white) **outer tail feathers**.

Water Pipit: resident in upland areas in extreme south-east of region, wintering in small numbers at wet localities elsewhere north to southern Britain and Low Countries. Markedly paler, greyer and more uniform than Rock Pipit. **White outer tail feathers** and prominent **pale stripe over eye**. In summer plumage unstreaked on under-parts with a marked pinkish flush.

streaked rump

RED-THROATED PIPIT

summer

winter

Rock Pipit

Scandinavian Rock Pipit

Rock

Water

Water Pipit winter

Water Pipit summer

ROCK / WATER PIPIT

15 cm (6 in.)

WAGTAILS (PASSERIFORMES; MOTACILLIDAE) *Slim, long-tailed, ground-living birds with long slender legs used for running or walking. Plumage bright or striking. Males more colourful than females. Immatures and winter males resemble females.*

Pied/White Wagtail *Motacilla alba*: 18 cm (7″)   Resident in British Isles and France, summer visitor throughout remainder of region. Inhabits open country, usually closely associated with farmland, human habitation or fresh water. Pied Wagtail is confined to British Isles, White Wagtail occurring elsewhere in region. Immatures can show yellowish tinge around face but never on remainder of under-parts. Runs rapidly, chasing insects on ground or sometimes fluttering into air to catch flying food. Tail-wagging and **back-and-forth movements of head while walking** are distinctive. Flight strongly undulating. Gregarious, particularly at roost outside breeding season. White Wagtail has grey, not black, rump in all plumages and ages; adult male has grey back and black of head does not join with black of breast. Voice: typical call note a rather high-pitched '*tchiswick*' with rather twittering song a series of these calls.

Grey Wagtail *Motacilla cinerea*: 18 cm (7″)   Resident throughout region except Scandinavia where summer visitor to extreme south only. Inhabits freshwater sites breeding near running water particularly in upland areas and moving to more lowland sites in winter months. **Longer tailed than other wagtails.** Always shows yellow on under-parts but lacks yellowish or greenish tinge to back and head. Usually solitary, readily perching on vegetation overhanging water or on prominent perch in water. Tail movement more definite than other wagtails and very obvious. Voice: call distinctive single '*tsit*'; insignificant treble-noted song rarely heard.

Yellow Wagtail: *Motacilla flava*: 16·5 cm (6·5″)   Summer visitor throughout region except northernmost Scotland and Ireland. Inhabits open areas of farmland and grassland, usually associated with fresh water. Smaller and shorter tailed than other wagtails. Under-parts generally yellow, **upper-parts distinctly greenish**. Very gregarious outside breeding season, closely associated with feeding cattle. Occurs in region in three distinct races, only the males in summer plumage being distinguishable and only by head coloration. Voice: distinctive '*tsweep*' flight call, infrequently heard trilling song.
Yellow Wagtail: confined to British Isles. Head yellow-green with yellow stripe over eye and yellow throat.
Grey-headed Wagtail: confined to northern Scandinavia. Head dark grey with blackish patch behind eye, no stripe over eye.
Blue-headed Wagtail: occurs in remainder of region. Head bluish-grey, slightly darker behind eye with white stripe over eye and varying extent of white on chin.
Note: variants and intermediates between these races do occur.

PIED/WHITE WAGTAIL

Pied Wagtail ♂

White Wagtail ♂

♀ Pied Wagtail

imm

GREY WAGTAIL

♂ summer

♀

& ♂ winter

imm

♀

Yellow Wagtail ♂

♂ Blue-headed Wagtail

Grey-headed Wagtail ♂

YELLOW WAGTAIL

15 cm (6 in.)

SHRIKES (PASSERIFORMES; LANIIDAE)   *Predatory birds with aggressive habits; possessing strong legs, hooked bill and rather long tails. Regularly sit on exposed perches in open country, particularly favouring overhead wires. Sexes similar (except Red-backed Shrike), immatures brown, mottled or scaly.*

Great Grey Shrike *Lanius excubitor*: 24 cm (9·5")   Summer visitor to central and northern Scandinavia, winter visitor to Scotland, eastern England and western France, absent Ireland; resident throughout remainder of region. Inhabits open areas with scattered trees and bushes. **Largest shrike**, differing from LESSER GREY SHRIKE in lack of black on forehead, pure white under-parts and longer tail with more extensive white areas. **When perched** usually adopts **forward-leaning position**, unlike upright stance of Lesser Grey Shrike. Tail in continual motion while perched, usually in a circular pattern. Flight undulating and low, swooping upwards to perch. Regularly hovers. Prey is impaled on thorns to form 'larder'. Voice: harsh, chattering cry, all shrikes sounding similar.

Lesser Grey Shrike *Lanius minor*: 20 cm (8")   Summer visitor to south of region. Inhabits open heath and scrub with scattered tall trees. Differs from larger GREAT GREY SHRIKE in proportionately shorter tail, **broad black forehead**, no white stripe over eye, pinkish flush to under-parts and reduced white in wing. **Wings** longer than Great Grey Shrike, **extending well down tail**. Sits more upright than Great Grey Shrike. Flight more direct, often gliding; hovers regularly. Voice: see Great Grey Shrike.

Woodchat Shrike *Lanius senator*: 17 cm (6·75")   Summer visitor to south of region. Inhabits open areas of scrub and heath with isolated tall trees and bushes. Plumage of adults distinctive from all other shrikes. **Immatures** resemble immature RED-BACKED SHRIKE but are distinguished by a paler grey appearance and have **pale areas on wings, shoulders and rump** where adults have white. Habits closely resemble other shrikes, particularly Red-backed, and although makes use of exposed perches will more readily sit amongst foliage in hidden positions than other shrikes. Voice: see Great Grey Shrike, but song rather more musical than other shrikes.

Red-backed Shrike *Lanius collurio*: 17 cm (6·75")   Summer visitor north to southern England and central Scandinavia. Inhabits heath and downland with isolated bushes and trees. Adult distinctive. Immatures browner than immature WOOD-CHAT SHRIKE and more uniform, lacking pale areas. Flight low and undulating, swooping upwards to perch. Tail moves in circular pattern when perched. Drops to ground for food or flies upwards to catch flying food. Prey often impaled on thorns to form 'larder'. Will sit motionless in crouching position for long periods when easily overlooked. Voice: see Great Grey Shrike; also has quiet warbling song.

GREAT GREY
SHRIKE

LESSER
GREY
SHRIKE

WOODCHAT
SHRIKE

ad

imm

♂

imm

♀

RED-BACKED
SHRIKE

15 cm (6 in.)

WAXWINGS (PASSERIFORMES; BOMBYCILLIDAE)

Waxwing *Bombycilla garrulus*: 18 cm (7″)   Resident in northern Scandinavia, winter visitor throughout remainder of region but numbers and extent of movement westwards in winter months varying greatly from year to year. Inhabits wide variety of open woodland in breeding season. In winter months closely associated with berried shrubs and trees in parks, gardens, etc. Immediately identified by distinctive plumage, behaviour, and **prominent crest**. Often tame and confiding. Very STARLING-like in flight, but rounder, plumper bodied. Very gregarious, large parties often completely stripping a collection of berry-bearing bushes. Active and acrobatic when feeding, often hanging upside down from outer twigs, at other times rather immobile. Drinks regularly and frequently. Voice: single Redwing-like *'tseep'*.

STARLINGS (PASSERIFORMES; STURNIDAE)   *Familiar, highly gregarious birds, closely associated with man. Noisy and quarrelsome, very active, mainly ground feeding. Sexes, winter and summer plumages similar, immatures paler and browner.*

Starling *Sturnus vulgaris*: 21·5 cm (8·5″)   Summer visitor to central and northern Scandinavia, resident throughout remainder of region. Inhabits wide variety of areas, ranging from woodland and open parks and gardens to town and city centres. Probably most abundant land-bird of region. Confusion is possible with BLACKBIRD (p. 174), but distinguished by shorter tail, **iridescent plumage** and walking, not hopping. Flight strong and direct, with characteristic **triangular shape of wings**. Will hawk for flying insects when action resembles feeding swallows. Highly gregarious, particularly outside breeding season when roosts of many thousands may occur in woods, reed-beds or buildings in town centres. Voice: very vocal with wide variety of chattering and whistling notes. Regularly mimics other species or familiar sounds.

Rose-coloured Starling *Sturnus roseus*: 21·5 cm (8·5″)   Rather scarce but annual visitor to region from south-east Europe. Inhabits drier, more open areas than STARLING. Adult birds distinctive, **immatures** similar to immature Starling but generally paler with **pale legs** and **yellow base to bill**. Habits similar to Starling. Very gregarious, often mixed with Starlings, particularly if feeding near livestock. Voice: similar to Starling but slightly more musical, less harsh.

WAXWING

STARLING

winter

moulting

summer

imm

imm

ad

ROSE-COLOURED STARLING

15 cm (6 in.)

FINCHES (PASSERIFORMES; FRINGILLIDAE) *Bill short, stout or conical; seed-eating birds, often very brightly coloured and highly gregarious in winter months. Males more brightly coloured than females, immatures resemble females. Winter and summer plumages similar.*

Hawfinch *Coccothraustes coccothraustes*: 18 cm (7″) Resident throughout region north to northern England and southern Scandinavia. Inhabits areas of open and mixed woodlands, parks, large gardens, etc. Largest wide-distributed finch of region with **massive bill** and **short tail** giving characteristic, rather top-heavy outline in flight. The huge bill is used to crack fruit stones. Rather retiring and easily overlooked in upper foliage of trees, but forms flocks in winter when more easily observed. Flight rather bouncy when white on wings and tail clearly visible. Feeds mainly in tree canopy, but will come to ground where moves with very upright carriage. Voice: most frequently used note a short '*ptik*' or high-pitched '*sip*'.

Greenfinch *Carduelis chloris*: 14·5 cm (5·75″) Resident throughout region north to central Scandinavia. Inhabits almost all areas except dense woodland and forests, common in parks and gardens, frequenting farmland in winter months. Largest of the yellow or greenish finches of the region, **plump** and rather stout bodied with **rather neckless appearance**. Flight less deeply undulating than many finches. During summer months feeds mainly in trees and bushes, becoming more of a ground feeder in winter when highly gregarious and favouring very exposed areas, often mixed with other finches. Voice: twittering song delivered from perch or in fluttering bat-like display flight. Most typical breeding-season note a very nasal, drawn-out '*dssweee*'; also uses a canary-like flight call.

Goldfinch *Carduelis carduelis*: 12 cm (4·75″) Resident throughout region except Scandinavia where summer visitor to south. Inhabits wide variety of sites, particularly favouring gardens, parks and areas of waste land. Plumage of adults highly distinctive, immatures retaining adult **yellow wing patterning**. Flight very bouncy, almost dancing. Rather tame and confiding in suburban areas, often nesting close to houses. Regularly seen on or near ground, feeding on seed-heads of thistle and other tall plants where very agile and acrobatic, hanging in tit-like manner (p. 164). Gregarious in winter months, often mixed with LINNET flocks (p. 212). Voice: most regularly used call a distinctive, liquid, tinkling series of notes.

HAWFINCH

ad

imm

GREENFINCH

♀

♂

15 cm (6 in.)

imm

ad

GOLDFINCH

FINCHES (PASSERIFORMES; Fringillidae)

Linnet *Acanthis cannabina*: 13·5 cm (5·25″)   Resident through-out region north to southern Scandinavia and summer visitor to central Scandinavia. Inhabits areas of low, open cover, such as heaths, downs, etc. Particularly favours gorse. Regularly moves to farmland or coastal sites in winter months. Differs from REDPOLL and TWITE in having dark bill and very prominent **white flashes in wing and tail**. Generally keeps to low perches and regularly on ground. Flight undulating but slightly less bouncy than GOLDFINCH (p. 210). Very gregarious, almost colonial when breeding and regularly mixed with other species in winter.Voice: series of rapidly twittering notes extended to form rather musical canary-like song.

Twite *Acanthis flavirostris*: 13·5 cm (5·25″)   Summer visitor to central and northern Scandinavia, resident southern Scandinavia, northern England, Scotland and Ireland, wintering in coastal areas of southern North Sea. Inhabits open upland, heaths and moors, becoming more coastal on salt marshes in winter months. Upland replacement of LINNET from which it differs in having unmarked buff throat, **yellow bill in winter** and **pinkish rump in male**. Habits closely resemble Linnet, with which it regularly mixes in winter months. Voice: rather Linnet-like but also has distinctive disyllabic nasal note.

Redpoll *Acanthis flammea*: 13 cm (5″)   Summer visitor to northern Scandinavia, resident southern Scandinavia and British Isles, winter visitor elsewhere in region. Inhabits mixed woodlands, large gardens, parks, etc. Closely associated with water in winter months. Distinguished from LINNET and TWITE by combination of **black chin** and **red forehead** and shorter-tailed appearance. Very active, feeding from seeds in tit-like manner (p. 164). Gregarious, flocks in very close association, regularly mixed with SISKIN (p. 214) to feed on alders in winter. Occurs in three races, those from British Isles (Lesser Redpoll) being very slightly smaller and slightly darker brown, those from Scandinavia (Mealy Redpoll) being slightly larger and paler with whiter rump and bars on wings. An occasional winter visitor to the region is the Greenland Redpoll which is larger, darker and slightly heavier billed than the other two races. Voice: uses a continual twittering note and a distinctive string of rather harsh, rapidly given notes in flight '*chur-chur-chur-chur*'.

Arctic Redpoll *Acanthis hornemanni*: 13 cm (5″)   Winter visitor to northern Scandinavia, southern limit of winter range varying from year to year. Inhabits arctic tundras and coastal areas. Distinctly paler than REDPOLL with **clear white rump** and very white, almost unstreaked under-parts showing pinkish flush. Paler on head and wing markings. Habits as Redpoll. Voice: similar to Redpoll but flight call said to be less rapid.

LINNET

♀   ♂

TWITE

♀   ♂

Mealy
Redpoll ♀   Mealy
Redpoll ♂

REDPOLL

♂   Lesser
Redpoll ♂

Greenland

♀

ARCTIC REDPOLL ♂

15 cm (6 in.)

FINCHES (PASSERIFORMES; FRINGILLIDAE)

Siskin *Carduelis spinus*: 12 cm (4·75″) Resident in southern Scandinavia, Scotland and Ireland, absent northern Scandinavia, winter visitor elsewhere. Inhabits areas associated with coniferous trees, either open sites or mixed woodlands. Small, yellow-rumped, greenish-yellow finch, differing from SERIN by **yellow flashes in tail. Bill pointed**, tail rather short. Typical bouncing flight action. Rarely comes to ground, feeding in trees, but increasingly visiting feeders at bird-tables in winter months. Gregarious when not breeding. Often in mixed flocks with REDPOLLS (p. 212) and feeds on alders in winter. Voice: twittering musical song delivered in fluttering display flight. Distinctive drawn-out *'tesw'* flight call.

Citril Finch *Serinus citrinella*: 12 cm (4·75″) Resident in extreme south-east of region. Inhabits coniferous forests in upland areas, moving to more open sites in winter months. Distinguished from other yellow-green finches by **grey on nape and sides of breast**, greenish-yellow rump and lack of yellow flashes in tail (but see SERIN). Gregarious, spending much of time on ground or low perches. Typical bouncing flight recalls GOLDFINCH (p. 210). Voice: song resembles Siskin, usually given in display flight. Rather nasal flight call.

Serin *Serinus serinus*: 11·5 cm (4·5″) Summer visitor north to English Channel and southern Scandinavia, but range spreading northwards. Inhabits wide variety of sites from open woodland, parks, gardens, orchards to towns, etc. Smallest finch of region, with roundish appearance, **short conical bill** and shortish tail. **Bright yellow rump**. Distinguished from SISKIN by lack of yellow in tail and no black on head. Typical undulating flight. Although closely associated with trees, readily comes to ground to feed. Very gregarious, even nesting in loose colonies. Voice: very vocal; flight call distinctive, a trilling, rather rapid *'trill-ill-ill-it'*. Song rather jingling, said to resemble Corn Bunting (p. 220) and delivered from high perch or in fluttering display flight.

SISKIN

♀

♂

CITRIL FINCH

♀

♂

15 cm (6 in.)

♀

♂

SERIN

FINCHES (PASSERIFORMES; FRINGILLIDAE)

Bullfinch *Pyrrhula pyrrhula*: 15 cm (6″)   Resident throughout region except northernmost Scandinavia where absent. Inhabits wide variety of sites, ranging from woodland, parks, gardens to suburban areas, particularly favouring orchards and closely associated with conifers in more northern sites. All plumages distinctive with **prominent white rump**, particularly noticeable in flight. Stout, conical, all-black bill and very plump appearance. Rather retiring, rarely leaving cover and never coming to ground. Particularly attracted to fruit buds. Occurs in pairs throughout the year, rarely flocking. Voice: distinctive, far-carrying, low-pitched *'peuw'* note. Also has rather feeble song.

Chaffinch *Fringilla coelebs*: 15 cm (6″)   Summer visitor to central and northern Scandinavia, resident elsewhere in region. Inhabits wide variety of woodland sites, parks and gardens, moving to more open areas in winter months. Commonest finch of region, regularly feeds on ground, both amongst trees and in more open situations. Typical undulating flight when **white shoulder flashes** very conspicuous. Gregarious when not breeding, flocks often composed of only one sex and mixed with other finches. Voice: song short but loud and travelling down the scale with a final flourish; most regular call notes *'pink'* and *'chup'*, the latter used in flight.

Brambling *Fringilla montifringilla*: 14·5 cm (5·75″)   Summer visitor to Scandinavia, winter visitor throughout remainder of region. Inhabits mainly birchwoods in breeding season, occurring in more open country during winter months. General shape and form resembles CHAFFINCH with peak-headed appearance, but immediately distinguished by **prominent white rump, orange breast and shoulders**. Ground feeding, closely associated with beech woods in winter, when gregarious and in mixed flocks with Chaffinches. Flight and movement similar to Chaffinch, but perhaps slightly more erratic. Voice: commonest note a drawn-out nasal call rather similar to Greenfinch (p. 210).

BULLFINCH

♂
♀

CHAFFINCH

♀
♂

BRAMBLING

♂ summer

♂ winter

♀

15 cm (6 in)

FINCHES (PASSERIFORMES; FRINGILLIDAE)

Scarlet or **Common Rosefinch** *Carpodacus erythrinus*: 14·5 cm (5·75″)   Summer visitor to southern Scandinavia although western limit of breeding range varies from year to year. Inhabits variety of sites ranging from woodlands and forest to garden and scrub. Only rosefinch of region, generally smaller than CROSSBILL and GROSBEAK. Amount of red in plumage of male is highly variable. Females and immatures are rather like slim buntings (p. 220) with pale wing-bars. **Bill rather conical** and bird looks **plump and round with neckless appearance**. Tail distinctly forked although most finches show notched tail. Flight undulating. Largely ground feeding. Voice: song a far-carrying piping, also using a disyllabic piping call note.

Pine Grosbeak *Pinicola enucleator*: 20 cm (8″)   Resident in northern Scandinavia extending to southern Scandinavia in winter months. Inhabits birch and coniferous woodland. Largest finch of region. General appearance similar to CROSSBILL but mandibles uncrossed and tail very much longer. **Bill heavy, very deep**. Moves and feeds through trees in manner of Crossbill, but comes to ground readily. Gregarious in winter, often tame and confiding. Voice: a variety of high-pitched whistles, usually in groups of three.

Crossbill *Loxia curvirostra*: 16·5 cm (6·5″)   Resident throughout region but western extent of breeding varies greatly from year to year. Inhabits coniferous woodlands. Commonest crossbill of region. Difficult to distinguish from scarcer PARROT CROSSBILL but smaller, with less deep bill. Tail short and markedly forked. Active and acrobatic when **feeding on pine cones**, silhouette distinctive, appearance rather parrot-like, often very tame. Rarely comes to ground except for drinking at regularly used sites. Voice: very distinctive metallic '*chip chip*' flight call. Song also metallic and rather bell-like.

Parrot Crossbill *Loxia pytyopsittacus*: 17 cm (6·75″)   Resident in central and southern Scandinavia. Inhabits coniferous forests. Larger than the commoner CROSSBILL, with more **massive bill** and larger head giving a **top-heavy appearance**. Otherwise plumage similar to Crossbill. Rarely in mixed parties with other crossbills, and usually in smaller groups than those species. Habits as Crossbill but preference for pines whereas Crossbill prefers spruce. Voice: similar to Crossbill but deeper.

Two-barred Crossbill *Loxia leucoptera*: 14·5 cm (5·75″) More eastern bird, appearing in southern Scandinavia as migrant in some years. Smallest crossbill of region with **conspicuous double white wing-bars**, similar in appearance to CHAFFINCH (p. 216). Bill smaller, more slender than other crossbills. Habits similar to CROSSBILL but prefers feeding in larches. Voice: similar persistent call as Crossbill, but less metallic; song twittering and rather unCrossbill-like.

218

SCARLET or COMMON ROSEFINCH

♀ ♂

PINE GROSBEAK

♀ ♂

imm

CROSSBILL

♂

imm ♀

PARROT CROSSBILL

♂

TWO-BARRED CROSSBILL

♀ ♂

15 cm (6 in.)

BUNTINGS (PASSERIFORMES; EMBERIZIDAE) *Basically ground-living finches, inhabiting areas of low scrub in more open country than true finches. Bills rather conical and deep based. Males generally more strikingly marked than females; immatures resemble females. Winter and summer plumages similar.*

Corn Bunting *Emberiza calandra*: 18 cm (7″) Resident throughout region north to southern Scandinavia. Inhabits dry open farmland and scrub areas, particularly in coastal localities. Largest and most nondescript of buntings, males and females identical. **Rather plump** in appearance, **sitting in very upright position**, often with head pointing upwards. **Flight heavy** and undulating, regularly **with legs dangling**. Gregarious and frequently polygamous. Voice: unmusical jangling song said to resemble shaking of a bunch of keys. Flight call a rather liquid '*tsiip*'.

Yellowhammer *Emberiza citrinella*: 16·5 cm (6·5″) Summer visitor to northern Scandinavia, resident throughout remainder of region. Inhabits farmland, heath, scrub and woodland clearings. All ages and plumages differ from scarcer CIRL BUNTING in having **chestnut rump**. Rather long-tailed effect in flight. Feeds almost exclusively on ground, but perches readily on bushes where tail is occasionally flicked. Typical undulating finch-like flight. Gregarious when not breeding, often mixed with other finches and buntings. Voice: familiar song, well-known by the phrase 'a little bit of bread and no cheese'. Call note a single '*spit*'.

Cirl Bunting *Emberiza cirlus*: 16·5 cm (6·5″) Resident in France and southern England. Inhabits areas of farmland with hedgerows and open scrub. Head plumage of male distinctive, females and immatures closely resemble YELLOWHAMMER but with **olive-brown** (not chestnut) **rump**. General appearance more compact, not as long as Yellowhammer. Gregarious, often mixed with Yellowhammers in winter, but more frequently on taller trees. Voice: similar to Yellowhammer, call note rather higher pitched, and song without final flourish, resembling Lesser Whitethroat.

Ortolan Bunting *Emberiza hortulana*: 16·5 cm (6·5″) Summer visitor throughout region except northernmost Scandinavia and British Isles. Inhabits farmland and open country with scattered trees and bushes. All plumages show **pale eye-rings** and **pinkish bill**. Flight and movements typical of bunting but rather shy and secretive. Easily disturbed when usually flies some distance before resettling. Voice: song a series of musical '*tseu*' notes; typical call note a single '*twit*', rather liquid in quality and, once known, a useful identification feature.

CORN BUNTING

♀

♂

YELLOWHAMMER

♀

CIRL BUNTING

♂

♀

♂

imm

ORTOLAN BUNTING

15 cm (6 in.)

BUNTINGS (PASSERIFORMES; EMBERIZIDAE)

Rock Bunting *Emberiza cia*: 16 cm (6·25″) Resident in extreme south and east of region. Inhabits stony or rocky upland areas or sparsely vegetated hillsides. Flight and behaviour similar to YELLOWHAMMER (p. 220), but almost **completely ground living** except when using trees or bushes for song posts. Regularly flicks tail showing white outer feathers, and flutters wings while singing. Voice: single, rather sharp, typical bunting flight call, and buzzing, rather simple song somewhat similar to Reed Bunting.

Rustic Bunting *Emberiza rustica*: 14·5 cm (5·75″) Summer visitor to northern Scandinavia. Inhabits upland forest areas, usually associated with wet or damp sites. Head pattern of breeding male distinctive. In all plumages shows **rust-coloured breast-band**. Frequently raises crown feathers to give peaked appearance to head. Very active, rarely far from ground, regularly feeding around tree roots. Voice: flight call a sharp 'tic'. Song rather short, in some ways reminiscent of Dunnock.

Little Bunting *Emberiza pusilla*: 13·5 cm (5·25″) Summer visitor to northernmost Scandinavia, inhabiting tundra scrubland. Smallest bunting of region with characteristic **chestnut-rufous cheeks**. Generally slimmer than other buntings and noticeably shorter tailed. Retiring and easily overlooked. Feeds on ground with rather shuffling action. Very hunchbacked. Flicks and fans tail in manner of REED BUNTING. Gregarious, often mixed with parties of other ground-living birds. Voice: a single 'tic' call note, very Robin-like, and jingly, simple song.

Reed Bunting *Emberiza schoeniclus*: 15 cm (6″) Summer visitor to central and northern Scandinavia, resident throughout remainder of region. Inhabits open areas associated with fresh water and marshes but increasing tendency to move to drier farmland and scrub-type habitats, even starting to visit bird-tables in suburban areas during winter months. Commonest and most familiar bunting of region. Black head with white collar and moustachial streak of male distinctive. **Moustachial streak** well marked in all plumages. Prominent white outer tail feathers readily seen as bird continually flicks and spreads tail and flutters wings. Rarely high up in vegetation, preferring to cling to stems of reeds, willows, etc., close to ground. Semi-gregarious in winter months, parties of all males often forming in early spring. Voice: monotonous, unmusical song, usually of four notes and can be rendered as 'burp burp burp pardon'. Call note rather Yellow Wagtail-like (p. 204).

ROCK BUNTING

♀

♂

winter ♂

summer ♂

RUSTIC BUNTING

♀

LITTLE BUNTING

summer ♂

winter ♂

♀

REED BUNTING

15 cm (6 in.)

BUNTINGS (PASSERIFORMES; EMBERIZIDAE)

Lapland Bunting *Calcarius lapponicus*: 15 cm (6″) Summer visitor to central and northern Scandinavia, wintering in coastal areas of southern North Sea. Inhabits tundra areas during breeding season, coastal sites and moorland in winter months. Rather plump-bodied, purely ground-living bunting with very broad-based wings. Gregarious in winter months, often mixing with SKYLARK (p. 154) or other buntings and finches. Flight more undulating than similarly shaped SNOW BUNTING. Voice: **call**, a **characteristic** trilling *'ticky-ticky-teu'*. Song is short but sweet and somewhat resembles Skylark.

Snow Bunting *Plectrophenax nivalis*: 16·5 cm (6·5″) Summer visitor to central and northern Scandinavia, wintering in coastal areas throughout remainder of region. Inhabits bare mountains and tundras in breeding season, moving to coastal marshes and salt-flats in winter months. Very stocky, plump-bodied bunting, similar to LAPLAND BUNTING in build and outline. Very broad-based wings. Purely ground living. Plumage of breeding male distinctive, immatures and females always show **pale under-parts** and **white areas on wings and tail**. Flight rapid, with strong undulations. Gregarious in winter but never mixes with other species. Voice: song, delivered from stony promontory, is loud and musical; call notes consist of distinctive bubbling twitter.

SPARROWS (PASSERIFORMES; PLOCEIDAE) *Rather dull-coloured finches with square-ended (not forked or cleft) tails. In species of region males resemble females (except House Sparrows); immatures, winter and summer plumages similar.*

Snow Finch *Montifringilla nivalis*: 18 cm (7″) Resident in extreme south-east of region. Inhabits stony upland areas, moving to lower sites in winter months when sometimes associated with human habitations. Flight pattern similar to SNOW BUNTING but lacking white on head or upper-parts. **Distribution** of two species prevent confusion. Completely ground living, perching very upright and regularly flicking tail. Voice: song, usually delivered in display flight, rather monotonous series of repeated calls.

LAPLAND BUNTING

♀

♂

♂

SNOW BUNTING
(winter)

♀

SNOW FINCH

ad

imm

15 cm (6 in.)

SPARROWS (PASSERIFORMES; PLOCEIDAE)

House Sparrow *Passer domesticus*: 14·5 cm (5·75"). Resident throughout region. Inhabits all areas associated with man, towns, villages and cultivated areas. Probably the most familiar small brown bird of region. Males distinctive, differing from TREE SPARROW by **grey crown**, extensive black bib and single white wing-bar. Females and immatures rather nondescript. Regularly perches on trees and buildings but mainly ground feeder where hops with frequent flicks of tail. Very communal. During breeding season often in noisy, bustling groups. Winter roosts often form in woodland, mixed with other species, particularly GREENFINCHES (p. 210). Voice: varied collection of chirping, cheeping and chattering notes.

Tree Sparrow *Passer montanus*: 14 cm (5·5") Resident throughout region north to central Scandinavia. Inhabits areas of woodland or open places with scattered trees. Less associated with man than HOUSE SPARROW but common on farmland. Sexes similar, differing from male House Sparrow in slightly smaller size, stockier appearance with shorter tail, **chestnut crown** and **black spot on white cheek**. Less confident in presence of man than House Sparrow. Cocks tail and droops wings more readily. Very active and gregarious, nesting in semi-colonies, flocks often mixed with other species in winter. Voice: typical flight call a rather hoarse *'chu-chu'* somewhat similar to Redpoll. Variety of other notes higher pitched than House Sparrow.

Rock Sparrow *Petronia petronia*: 14 cm (5·5") Resident in extreme south of region. Inhabits rocky or stony upland areas, rather scarce. Most closely resembles a rather pale, short-tailed female HOUSE SPARROW, with **head stripes**, **white spots on tail** and rather indistinct **yellow spot on breast**. Almost exclusively a bird of the ground, where moves about in manner of a lark (p. 154). Will occasionally perch on buildings. Very active and gregarious at all times, nesting in scattered colonies, occasionally mixed with House Sparrows. Voice: wide variety of typical sparrow-like notes, but also a rather characteristic single *'tut'* call and disyllabic *'pui-ee'* note.

HOUSE SPARROW

♂

♀

TREE SPARROW

ROCK SPARROW

ad

imm

15 cm (6 in.)

The birds described on the following pages are some of the more regularly occurring vagrants that visit the region, usually at times of migration, particularly in autumn and usually in immature or winter plumage.

Spectacled Eider *Somateria fischeri*: 54 cm (21·5″)   A bird of the high Arctic, occasionally appearing in northernmost Scandinavia in winter months. Males with green head and pale area around eye distinctive. Females similar to other female eiders (p. 44) but retain **pale, circular patch around eye** and feathers extending well down bill. In flight white back of male gives pattern similar to EIDER (p. 44). Compared with other eiders looks heavy and rather clumsy.

Ruddy Shelduck *Tadorna ferruginea*: 64 cm (25″)   A scarce visitor from south-east Europe although position very complicated by escapees from waterfowl collections. Somewhat similar species of shelduck are also kept in collection and confusion is possible. Shape and behaviour similar to SHEL-DUCK (p. 42) but more likely to be found on freshwater sites. In natural areas rarely seen singly, always in pairs or small parties. Swims readily but behaves more like goose, grazing and walking on fields. Rarely mixes with other waterfowl. Voice: loud ringing call similar to domestic goose.

American Wigeon *Anas americana*: 50 cm (20″)   A North American duck similar in build and shape to WIGEON (p. 34), differing in male by pinkish brown plumage with **green-and-white head pattern**. Female doubtfully distinguishable unless very close view obtained when rather greyer appearance of head and neck and pure white under-wing are distinctive. Habits as Wigeon but favours freshwater sites much more than that species. Voice: as Wigeon.

Surf Scoter *Melanitta perspicillata*: 56 cm (22″)   Scarce North American sea duck differing from other scoter (p. 42) by rather EIDER-like bill (p. 44) and distinctive distribution of **pale areas on head** of both sexes. Females lack white wing flash of VELVET SCOTER (p. 42). General habits resemble Velvet Scoter but in flight usually appears less heavy than that species. Often mixes in flocks with other sea ducks. Rarely close inshore and where occurring in some numbers does not apparently fly in line formation as other scoter. Voice: usually silent.

SPECTACLED
EIDER

♀

♂

RUDDY
SHELDUCK

♀

AMERICAN
WIGEON

♂

♀

♂

♀

SURF
SCOTER

15 cm (6 in.)

Terek Sandpiper *Xenus cinereus*: 23 cm (9″) Scarce visitor from eastern Europe, small numbers breeding annually in Finland. Inhabits mainly freshwater sites. Differs from all other small sandpipers (p. 102) by **thin, rather long, upturned bill**. Habits somewhat similar to COMMON SANDPIPER (p. 96), bobbing body in identical manner and with the same flicking wing action in flight. Usually solitary and relatively tame, allowing close approach. Voice: trilling flight call and single or disyllabic alarm note.

Wilson's Phalarope *Phalaropus tricolor*: 23 cm (9″) Scarce North American phalarope, larger and longer billed than other phalaropes (p. 108) and more inclined to run on land but swims readily. Flight pattern similar to WOOD SANDPIPER (p. 96). Very active, running with characteristic swaying movement and moving bill from side to side. Has been observed 'spinning' on land and in water. Voice: has variety of low, grunting calls.

Cream-coloured Courser *Cursorius cursor*: 27 cm (9″) Scarce vagrant from North Africa. Inhabits dry, open areas; in some ways resembling GOLDEN PLOVER (p. 90) but with **long legs** and **pointed, slightly decurved bill**. Moves with series of runs, and crouches but occasionally stands upright with stretched neck. Voice: generally silent.

Collared Pratincole *Glareola pratincola*: 25 cm (10″) Summer visitor to extreme south of Europe. Inhabits open areas of dried mud and sand, particularly at edges of freshwater sites. Wader-like on ground but very tern-like (p. 124) in flight with **long pointed wings**. Moves rapidly on ground in series of runs with body held horizontal. Highly gregarious, flocks often performing aerial manoeuvres and hawking communally for insects. Rather crepuscular. Voice: noisy, with variety of chattering notes. The Black-winged Pratincole, *Glareola nordmanni*, from south-east Europe and southern Asia, is an even rarer visitor to the region.

TEREK SANDPIPER

ad

imm

WILSON'S PHALAROPE

winter

summer

CREAM-COLOURED COURSER

ad

imm

COLLARED PRATINCOLE

ad

imm

Black-winged Pratincole

15 cm (6 in.)

RARITIES

Little Shearwater *Puffinus assimilis*: 27 cm (10·5″) Rare vagrant sea-bird from rocky Atlantic islands, most frequently recorded in western Ireland. A small version of MANX SHEARWATER (p. 20) differing by **blue feet** and **black of head not extending below eye**. Proportionately shorter winged than Manx Shearwater. Flight has less gliding than other shearwaters with rapid, fluttering wing-beats. Voice: similar to Manx Shearwater on breeding ground but less vocal.

American Bittern *Botaurus lentiginosus*: 66 cm (26″) Scarce vagrant from North America, inhabiting reed-beds, marshes and other wet areas. Smaller than BITTERN (p. 28) which it closely resembles but lacks black crown, has **black stripe down side of neck** and strongly mottled under-parts. Solitary. Habits similar to Bittern but more frequently occurring in open areas and consequently more easily observed. Most active at dusk and during night. Uses same 'freezing' attitude as Bittern. Voice: nasal trisyllabic flight note; breeding call unlikely to be heard in region.

Pallas's Sandgrouse *Syrrhaptes paradoxus*: 38 cm (15″) Scarce vagrant from Asia inhabiting open sandy or dry mud areas. In past years vast westward migrations have taken the birds to the Atlantic seaboard but none since the early years of the century. Rather striking plumage is only apparent at close range. General appearance is rather **like a long-tailed pigeon**, with swept-back wings and striking **black belly patch**. Very difficult to see when crouched and generally shy. Very short legs give waddling movement when walking with body very close to ground. Voice: single or double *'kack'* flight call.

Snow Goose *Anser caerulescens*: 74 cm (29″) Vagrant goose from arctic North America, occurs in two colour phases, the blue phase with dark body and wings and white phase with all-white plumage and black wing-tips. Usually mixed with other geese when occurring in region but escapees from water-fowl collections also occur. Voice: high-pitched single note or rapidly repeated series of notes.

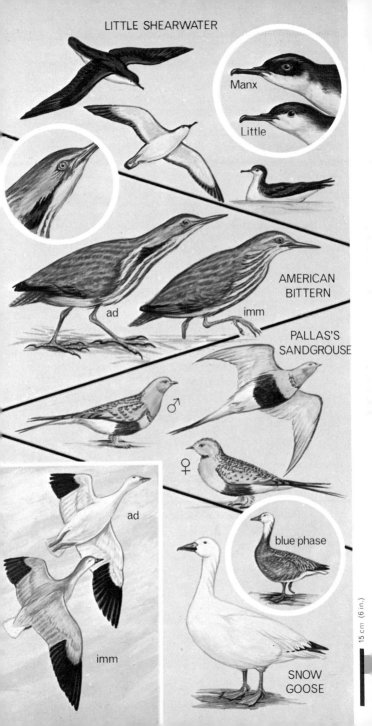

LITTLE SHEARWATER

Manx

Little

AMERICAN
BITTERN

ad

imm

PALLAS'S
SANDGROUSE

♂

♀

ad

imm

blue phase

SNOW
GOOSE

15 cm (6 in.)

RARITIES

Red-flanked Bluetail *Tarsiger cyanurus*: 14 cm (5·5″)   Occasional vagrant from breeding areas in Finland. Inhabits scrub areas associated with coniferous forests, often in damp locations. Rather REDSTART-like (p. 178) but with **blue tail** and **rufous colouring on flanks**. Generally shy, rapidly moving to cover if disturbed or creeping amongst undergrowth like ROBIN (p. 178) but will feed in manner of flycatchers (p. 198). Regularly jerks and flicks tail. Voice: song quiet with thrush-like quality, single Robin-like call note.

White's Thrush *Zoothera dauma*: 27 cm (11″)   Vagrant thrush from central and eastern Asia, larger than any of the regular thrushes of region. Only possible confusion is with immature MISTLE THRUSH (p. 172) from which it differs by **crescent-shaped markings** on both upper- and under-parts and golden, not greyish, general coloration. Striking **black-and-white under-wing** pattern is distinctive. Almost entirely ground living, running rather than hopping. Very undulating flight. Voice: Mistle Thrush-like call.

Rock Thrush *Monticola saxatilis*: 19 cm (7·5″)   Vagrant from breeding grounds in southern Europe. Inhabits open or rocky country with sparse vegetation. Males strikingly plumaged and unmistakable; females and immatures mottled but retaining **red tail**. Rather shy, and not very active, usually making for cover when observed. Feeds mainly on ground but perches readily on bushes, trees and buildings. Continual flicking movement of tail. Voice: Wheatear-like chacking note and clear, rather Blackbird-like (p. 174) song often delivered in flight.

Richard's Pipit *Anthus novaeseelandiae*: 18 cm (7″)   Rather scarce but almost annual vagrant from Siberia. Largest pipit (p. 200) to occur in region, in some ways rather reminiscent of a small thrush. Very **long pale legs** and **upright stance**, running rapidly. Very bold pattern on under-parts and warm brown on upper-parts distinguish this species from TAWNY PIPIT (p. 200). Flight wagtail-like (p. 204) and very undulating. Will perch on low bushes or promontories but rarely any height above ground. Voice: very distinct '*tr-r-rup*' flight call.

RED-FLANKED
BLUETAIL

♀

♂

under-
wing

WHITE'S THRUSH

ROCK THRUSH

♂

♀

RICHARD'S PIPIT

15 cm (6 in.)

River Warbler *Locustella fluviatilis*: 13 cm (5″) Vagrant from breeding grounds in eastern Europe. Inhabits wide variety of sites but usually closely associated with well-vegetated freshwater areas. Differs from similar-sized GRASSHOPPER WARBLER (p. 182) in having browner unstreaked upperparts and rather fine streakings on breast and throat. Habits much as Grasshopper Warbler, extremely secretive and rarely taking flight. Voice: song distinctive, much slower and less steady than Grasshopper Warbler, usually delivered from exposed perch and most frequent in late evening or during night.

Olivaceous Warbler *Hippolais pallida*: 13·5 cm (5·25″) Scarce vagrant from southern Europe. Inhabits wide variety of bushy and scrubland areas. Typical *Hippolais*-warbler shape (p. 186) but coloration of GARDEN WARBLER (p. 188), usually showing **pale eye-ring** and **whitish tips to tail feathers**. More closely resembles MELODIOUS WARBLER (p. 186) but lacks yellow or green coloration and has longer bill and flatter head. Skulking, but not particularly shy, mainly living in small trees rather than dense undergrowth or tall trees. Voice: call rather sparrow-like and song *Acrocephalus* warbler-like (p. 182), rarely delivered from exposed perch.

Pallas's Warbler *Phylloscopus proregulus*: 9 cm (3·5″) Rare vagrant to region from Asia. Smallest warbler to occur in region, equal in size to crests (p. 196). Only similar warbler is YELLOW-BROWED WARBLER (p. 196) from which it diäers in being brighter green and having **yellow crown stripe** bordered with dark green, two yellow wing-bars and **yellow rump**. Patterning of wings and rump very obvious when bird is hovering, a regular feeding habit. Very active, continually flitting through bushes and cover, behaving in very crest-like manner. Voice: quiet disyllabic note, rather similar to, but more dawn out than, call of Yellow-browed Warbler.

Alpine Accentor *Prunella collaris*: 18 cm (7″) Scarce vagrant from southern Europe. Inhabits stony or rocky upland areas with sparse vegetation. Considerably larger and stouter and more brightly coloured than DUNNOCK (p. 196). In flight shows **two pale wing-bars** and **white tip to tail**. Often flicks tail and flutters wings in manner of chats (p. 176). Moves along ground with typical shuffling action, rarely flying any distance when disturbed. Voice: song more musical than Dunnock and said to resemble a Skylark; call note rather harsh, a cross between Dunnock and House Sparrow.

RIVER WARBLER

OLIVACEOUS WARBLER

PALLAS'S WARBLER

ALPINE ACCENTOR

15 cm (6 in.)

RARITIES

Yellow-breasted Bunting *Emberiza aureola*: 14 cm (5·5″)
Scarce vagrant from eastern and northern Europe. Inhabits
areas of open wood and scrubland. Smallest of the yellow-
coloured buntings (p. 220) to occur in region. Male with very
distinctive plumage, female rather like small female YELLOW-
HAMMER (p. 220) differing by having unstreaked breast and
pale stripes on head. Gregarious, even nesting in loose colonies,
flocking in large groups in winter months. Breeding range is
slowly spreading westward. Voice: song loud and similar to
Ortolan Bunting (p. 220); call note a typical bunting-like
'*tsip*'.

Red-headed Bunting *Emberiza bruniceps*: 16·5 cm (6·5″)
Status in north-western Europe doubtful. Bird originates from
Asia but large numbers imported as cage-birds and most
records probably refer to escapees. Perhaps some genuine
vagrants occur. Inhabits scrubland, often associated with
fresh water. Male distinctively plumaged but extent and
intensity of red on head and breast is variable. Females
closely resemble female HOUSE SPARROW (p. 226) but under-
parts always show some trace of yellow, particularly on belly
and under tail. Habits similar to CORN BUNTING (p. 220). Voice:
variety of musical, whistling, harsh notes.

Black-headed Bunting *Emberiza melanocephala*: 16·5 cm
(6·5″)   Scarce vagrant from south-east Europe. Inhabits open
areas of woodland, scrub and gardens. Male distinctive with
black head and yellow under-parts and chestnut back.
Female closely resembles female RED-HEADED BUNTING but
shows some trace of **chestnut on rump**. Gregarious, large
flocks sometimes collecting on cultivated land. Habits similar
to CORN BUNTING (p. 220), often flying with dangling legs.
Voice: typical call note a bunting-like '*tzit*'.

YELLOW-BREASTED BUNTING

♂

♀

RED-HEADED BUNTING

♂

♀

winter

♂

♀

BLACK-HEADED BUNTING

15 cm (6 in.)

Check List/Table of Occurrence

The following list provides only a general guide to which species occur where at a particular time of year. It is impossible on such a table to detail specific geographical limits for various times of the year and the information should only be used as a general indication of a species' distribution in our region. More detailed information on distribution will be found amongst the books suggested for further reading on p. 263.

X indicates that the species is found in the winter months

O indicates that the species is found in the summer months
* indicates that the species is found throughout the year
m indicates that the species is found as a migrant moving from summer or winter quarters
(N), (S), (E), (W) indicate North, South, East, West—some guide to the part of the area involved when not found throughout
The space provided under 'Check List' is to enable you to record your own sightings of the various species.

PP	SPECIES	ENGLAND & WALES	SCOTLAND	IRELAND	FRANCE	GERMANY & BENELUX	SCANDI-NAVIA	CHECK LIST
16	Black-throated Diver	X	*		X	m	*	
	Great Northern Diver	X	X	X	X		X(W)	
	White-billed Diver			*(N); X(S)			X(N)	
	Red-throated Diver	X	*	*(N); X(S)	X	X	*	
18	Great Crested Grebe	*	*	*	*	*	*(S)	
	Red-necked Grebe	X(E)	X(E)		X(N)	O(E)	*(S)	
	Slavonian Grebe	X	*	X	X(N&W)	X(N)	*	
	Black-necked Grebe	X	*		*	*	O(S)	
	Little Grebe	*	*	*	*	*	*(S)	

PP	SPECIES	ENGLAND & WALES	SCOTLAND	IRELAND	FRANCE	GERMANY & BENELUX	SCANDI-NAVIA	CHECK LIST
20	Cory's Shearwater	m	m	m	m(N)			....
	Manx Shearwater	*	*	*	*(N)	m(N)	m(W)	....
	Great Shearwater	m	m	m	m(N&W)		m(W)	....
	Sooty Shearwater	m	m	m	m(N&W)			....
22	Fulmar	*	*	*	*(N)	*(N)	*(N)	....
	Wilson's Petrel				m(W)			....
	Storm Petrel	O(W)	O(W)	O(W)	O(W)			....
	Leach's Petrel	m(W)	O(N)	m	m(W)			....
24	Gannet	***	***	***	**	*(N)	*(W)	....
	Cormorant	***	***	***	**	*(N)	**	....
	Shag	***	***	***	*(N&W)		*(N&W)	....
26	Grey Heron	*	*	*	*	*	*(S&W)	....
	Purple Heron	m(S)			O(S)	O(N)		....
	Little Egret				O(S)			....
28	Squacco Heron				O(S)	O(N)		....
	Night Heron				O(S)	o		....
	Little Bittern				O	*		....
	Bittern	*			*		*(S)	....

PP	SPECIES	ENGLAND & WALES	SCOTLAND	IRELAND	FRANCE	GERMANY & BENELUX	SCANDINAVIA	CHECK LIST
30	White Stork				m	O	O(S)	
	Black Stork					O(E)		
	Spoonbill	m(S)			m(W)	O(N)		
32	Mallard	*	*	*	*	*	*(S); O(N)	
	Gadwall	*	*	*	*	*	O(S)	
34	Teal	*	*	*	*	*	*(S); O(N)	
	Garganey	O	*		O	O	O(S)	
	Wigeon	*	*	X	X	X	*(S); O(N)	
	Pintail	X	X	X	X	*	*(S); O(N)	
36	Shoveler	*	*	*	*	*	O(S)	
	Mandarin Duck	*	*					
	Red-crested Pochard	m(S)				*(N)	O(S)	
38	Scaup	X	X	X	X(N)	X(N)	O(N); X(S)	
	Tufted Duck	*	*	*	*	*	*(S); O(N)	
	Pochard	*	*	*	*	*	*(S)	
40	Ferruginous Duck	X	X	X	X(E)	O(E)		
	Goldeneye	X	X	X(N)	X	X	*(S); O(N)	
	Long-tailed Duck	X(E)				X(N)	*(N); X(S)	

PP	SPECIES	ENGLAND & WALES	SCOTLAND	IRELAND	FRANCE	GERMANY & BENELUX	SCANDINAVIA	CHECK LIST
42	Velvet Scoter	X(E)	X		X(N&W)	X(N)	*(N); X(S)	
	Common Scoter	*	**	**	*(N&W)	*(N)	*	
	Shelduck	*	**	**	*(N); X(W)	*(N)	*(S)	
44	Steller's Eider						X(N)	
	Eider	*	*	*	*(N)	*(N)	*	
	King Eider						X(N)	
46	Ruddy Duck	*(W)						
	Red-breasted Merganser	*(N); X(S)	**	*	X(N&W)	*(N)	*	
	Goosander	*(N); X(S)	**		X(E)	X	*(S); O(N)	
	Smew	X(S)			X(E)	X	X(S); O(N)	
48	Greylag Goose	*	*	*(N&E)		X(N)	*(S); O(N)	
	White-fronted Goose	X	X	X	X(N&W)	X(N)	m(S)	
	Lesser White-fronted Goose						O(N)	
50	Bean Goose	X	X		X(N&W)	X(N)	X(S); O(N)	
	Pink-footed Goose	X(E)	X			X(N)	X(S)	
	Bar-headed Goose						*	
	Egyptian Goose	*(E)						

PP	SPECIES	ENGLAND & WALES	SCOTLAND	IRELAND	FRANCE	GERMANY & BENELUX	SCANDI-NAVIA	CHECK LIST
52	Brent Goose	X	m	X	X(N&W)	X(N)	X(S)	
	Barnacle Goose		X	X		X(N)	*(S)	
	Canada Goose	*	*	*(N)		X(N)	*(S)	
54	Mute Swan	*	*	*	*	*	*(S)	
	Whooper Swan	X(N)	*	X		X(N)	X(S); O(N)	
	Bewick's Swan	X(S)	X	X	X(N)	X(N)	m(S)	
56	Golden Eagle		*				*	
	White-tailed Eagle					X	*(N); X(S)	
58	Spotted Eagle						m(S)	
	Lesser Spotted Eagle					O(N)		
60	Buzzard	*(N&W)	*		*	*	*(S); O(N)	
	Rough-legged Buzzard	X(E)	X(E)		X(N)	X	X(S); O(N)	
	Honey Buzzard	O(S)			O	O	O(S)	
62	Sparrowhawk	*	*	*	**	**	*(S); O(N)	
	Goshawk	m(S)				*	*(S); O(N)	
	Red Kite	*(W)			O(E)	O	O(S)	
	Black Kite				O(S)	O		

244

PP	SPECIES	ENGLAND & WALES	SCOTLAND	IRELAND	FRANCE	GERMANY & BENELUX	SCANDINAVIA	CHECK LIST
64	Marsh Harrier	*(S)			**	O	O(S)	
	Hen Harrier	*	*	*	**	*	*(S); O(N)	
	Montagu's Harrier	O(S)			O	O	O(S)	
66	Booted Eagle				O(S)			
	Short-toed Eagle				O(S)			
	Osprey	m	O		m	O(N)	O	
68	Hobby	O(S)		*	O	O	O(S)	
	Peregrine	*	*		*	*	**	
	Gyrfalcon							
	Saker Falcon					O(S)		
70	Merlin	*	*	*	X	X	O	
	Red-footed Falcon				*	m(E)	**	
	Kestrel	*	*	*	*	*	*(S); O(N)	
72	Red Grouse	*(N&W)	*	*			***	
	Ptarmigan		*				***	
	Black Grouse	*(W)	*		*(E)	*	***	
74	Capercaillie		*		*	*(S)	**	
	Hazelhen					*(S)	**	
	Pheasant	*	*	*		*	*(S)	

PP	SPECIES	ENGLAND & WALES	SCOTLAND	IRELAND	FRANCE	GERMANY & BENELUX	SCANDI-NAVIA	CHECK LIST
76	Red-legged Partridge	*(S&E)			*(W)	*		
	Partridge	*	*	*	*		*(S)	
	Quail	O	O	O	O	O	O(S)	
78	Golden Pheasant	*	*					
	Lady Amherst's Pheasant	*(S)						
	Silver Pheasant		*			*		
	Reeve's Pheasant	*(E)			*	*		
	Bobwhite					*		
	California Quail					*		
	Wild Turkey							
80	Spotted Crake	*(S)	O		*(W); O(E)	O	O(S)	
	Baillon's Crake				O(W)			
	Little Crake					O		
	Corncrake	O(N&W)	O	O	O	O	O(S)	
82	Water Rail	*	*	*	*		*(S)	
	Moorhen	*	*	*	*	*	*(S)	
	Coot	*	*	*	*	*	*(S)	
84	Crane				m	m	O	
	Great Bustard					*(N)		
	Little Bustard				O(S)			

PP	SPECIES	ENGLAND & WALES	SCOTLAND	IRELAND	FRANCE	GERMANY & BENELUX	SCANDI-NAVIA	CHECK LIST
86	Oystercatcher	*	*	*	*(N&W)	*(N)	*(S); O(N)	....
	Lapwing	*	*	*	*	*	*(S); O(N)	....
	Turnstone	X	X	X	X(N&W)	X(N)	O	....
88	Ringed Plover	*	*	*	X(N&W)	O(N)	O	....
	Little Ringed Plover	O	O(S)		O	O	O(S)	....
	Kentish Plover	m(S)			O(N&W)	O(N)	O(S)	....
90	Grey Plover	X	X	X	X(N&W)	X(N)	m	....
	Golden Plover	*(N&W)	*	*	X(N&W)	X(N)	O	....
	Dotterel		O			O(N)	O	....
92	Snipe	*	*	*	*	*	*(S); O(N)	....
	Great Snipe				m(E)	m	O	....
	Jack Snipe	X	X	X	X	m	O(N)	....
	Woodcock	*	*	*	*	*	*(S); O(N)	....
94	Curlew	*	*	*	*	*(N); O(S)	*(S); O(N)	....
	Whimbrel	m	O(N)	m	m	m	O	....
	Black-tailed Godwit	*(S)	m	X	X(W)	O(N)	O(S)	....
	Bar-tailed Godwit	X	X	X	X(N&W)	X(N)	O(N); X(S)	....
96	Green Sandpiper	X(S)	m	X(S)	X(W)	m	O(S)	....
	Wood Sandpiper	m	O(N)	m	m	O(N)	O	....
	Common Sandpiper	*(S); O(N)	O	O	*(W); O(E)	O	O	....

247

PP	SPECIES	ENGLAND & WALES	SCOTLAND	IRELAND	FRANCE	GERMANY & BENELUX	SCANDI-NAVIA	CHECK LIST
98	Redshank	*	*	*	X(N&W)	O	O	
	Spotted Redshank	X(S)	m	m	X(W)	m	O(N)	
	Greenshank	X(W)	O(N)	X	X(W)	m	O(N)	
102	Little Stint	m	m	m	m	m	m	
	Temminck's Stint	m(E)	m(E)		m	m	O(N)	
	Dunlin	*(N&W)	*	*	X(N&W)	*(N)	*(S); O(N)	
	Curlew Sandpiper	m	m	m	m	m	m	
104	Knot	X	X	X	X(N&W)	X(N)	m(S)	
	Purple Sandpiper	X	X	X	X(N)	X(N)	*(N); X(S)	
	Broad-billed Sandpiper					m	O(N)	
106	Ruff	X(S)	m	m	X(W)	O(N)	O	
	Avocet	*(S)			X(W)	O(N)	O(S)	
	Black-winged Stilt				O(W)			
	Stone Curlew	O(S)			O	m		
108	Sanderling	X	X	X	X(N&W)	X(N)	m	
	Grey Phalarope	m		m	m(N)	m(N)	m(S)	
	Red-necked Phalarope	m	O(N)	O(N)	m(N)	m(N)	O(N)	
110	Great Skua	m	O(N)	m	m(N&W)	m(N)	m	
	Pomarine Skua	m	m	m	m(N&W)			

248

PP	SPECIES	ENGLAND & WALES	SCOTLAND	IRELAND	FRANCE	GERMANY & BENELUX	SCANDI- NAVIA	CHECK LIST
110	Arctic Skua	m	O(N)	m	m(N&W)	m(N)	O	....
	Long-tailed Skua	m	m	m	m(W)	m(N)	O(N)	....
112	Ivory Gull						X(N)	....
	Great Black-backed Gull	*	*	**	*(N&W)	*(N)	*	....
	Lesser Black-backed Gull	*	O	**	*(N&W)	*(N)	O	....
114	Herring Gull	*	*	*	*	*	*	....
	Glaucous Gull	X(N&E)	X	X		X(N)	X	....
	Iceland Gull		X	X				....
116	Common Gull	*	*	*	*(N&W)	*(N)	*	....
	Mediterranean Gull				X(W)			....
	Black-headed Gull	*	*	*	*	*	*(S)	....
118	Little Gull	*(S)	X	m(W)	X(N&W)	*(N)	*(S)	....
	Sabine's Gull			*	m(W)			....
	Kittiwake	*	*		*(N&W)	X(N)	*(S); O(N)	....
120	Black Tern	O(S)		m	O	o	O(S)	....
	White-winged Black Tern					O(S)		....
	Whiskered Tern				O(S)			....
122	Gull-billed Tern	m(S)			m(N)	m(N)	O(S)	....

PP	SPECIES	ENGLAND & WALES	SCOTLAND	IRELAND	FRANCE	GERMANY & BENELUX	SCANDI-NAVIA	CHECK LIST
122	Caspian Tern	O(E)	O	O	O(N)	O(N)	O(E)	
	Sandwich Tern						O(S)	
124	Common Tern	O	O	O	O	O	O(S)	
	Arctic Tern	O(N)	O	O	O(N)	O(N)	O	
	Roseate Tern	O(N)	O(S)	O	O(N)			
	Little Tern	O	O	O	O(N&W)	O(N)	O(S)	
126	Razorbill	★	★	★	★	★	★	
	Guillemot	★	★	★	★	★	★	
	Brünnich's Guillemot						X(N)	
128	Little Auk	X(E)	X			X(N)	X(W)	
	Black Guillemot	★(N)	★	★			★	
	Puffin	O	O	O	O(N)	m(N)	★(S); O(N)	
130	Stock Dove	★	★	★	★	★	O(S)	
	Rock Dove		★	★	★(N)			
	Woodpigeon	★	★	★	★	★	★(N)	
132	Turtle Dove	O		m	O	O	O(S)	
	Collared Dove	★	★	★	★	★	★(S)	

250

PP	SPECIES	ENGLAND & WALES	SCOTLAND	IRELAND	FRANCE	GERMANY & BENELUX	SCANDINAVIA	CHECK LIST
134	Barn Owl	*	*	*	*	*	*(S)	
	Eagle Owl					*(S)	*	
	Snowy Owl		*(N)				*(N)	
136	Scops Owl				O(S)		*	
	Pygmy Owl						*(S)	
	Little Owl	*	*(S)		*	*		
	Tengmalm's Owl					*(E)	*	
138	Hawk Owl						*(N)	
	Great Grey Owl						*(N)	
	Ural Owl						*	
140	Tawny Owl	*	*		*	*	*(S)	
	Long-eared Owl	*	*	*	*	*	*(S)	
	Short-eared Owl	*	*	×	*	*	*(S); O(N)	
142	Cuckoo	O	O	O	O	O	O	
	Nightjar	O	O	O	O	O	O(S)	
	Kingfisher	*		*	*	*	*(S)	
144	Swift	O	O	O	O	O	O(S)	
	Alpine Swift				O(S)	O(S)		
	Bee-eater				m(S)	m(S)		

PP	SPECIES	ENGLAND & WALES	SCOTLAND	IRELAND	FRANCE	GERMANY & BENELUX	SCANDINAVIA	CHECK LIST
146	Roller	m(S)				O(E)		
	Hoopoe			m(S)	O	O	m(S)	
	Golden Oriole				O	O	O(S)	
148	Black Woodpecker				★(E)	★	★	
	Green Woodpecker	★	★(S)		★	★	★(S)	
	Grey-headed Woodpecker				★(S)	★(S)	★(S)	
150	Great Spotted Woodpecker	★	★		★	★	★	
	White-backed Woodpecker						★(S)	
	Middle Spotted Woodpecker				★	★	★(S)	
152	Three-toed Woodpecker				★	★	★	
	Lesser Spotted Woodpecker	★	★(S)				★	
	Wryneck	O(S)	m(E)	m(S)	O	O	O(S)	
154	Short-toed Lark				O(W)			
	Crested Lark				★	★	★(S)	
	Woodlark	★(S)			★	★(W); O(E)	O(S)	
	Skylark	★	★	★	★	★	★(S); O(N)	
	Shore Lark	X(E)			X(N)	X(N)	X(S); O(N)	

PP	SPECIES	ENGLAND & WALES	SCOTLAND	IRELAND	FRANCE	GERMANY & BENELUX	SCANDINAVIA	CHECK LIST
166	Siberian Tit						*	
	Marsh Tit	*			*	*	*(S)	
	Willow Tit	*	*(S)		*(E)	*	*	
	Long-tailed Tit	*	*	*	*	*	*(S)	
168	Penduline Tit				*	*(E)		
	Nuthatch	*				*	*(S)	
	Bearded Tit	*(S)				*(N)		
170	Wallcreeper					*(S)		
	Treecreeper	*	*	*		*(E)		
	Short-toed Treecreeper				*	*		
	Wren	**	**	**	*	*	*(S)	
	Dipper	**	**	**	*	*	**	
172	Mistle Thrush	**	**	**	**	*	*(S); O(N)	
	Song Thrush	**	**			O	O	
	Redwing	X	X	X	X	X	O(N); X(S)	
174	Fieldfare	X	X	X	X	*(E); X(W)	*(S); O(N)	
	Ring Ousel	O(N&W)	O	O(N)	m	m	O	
	Blackbird	*	*	*	*	*	*(S)	

PP	SPECIES	ENGLAND & WALES	SCOTLAND	IRELAND	FRANCE	GERMANY & BENELUX	SCANDI-NAVIA	CHECK LIST
176	Wheatear	O	O	O	O	O	O	
	Stonechat	*	*	*	*(N); O(S)	O		
	Whinchat	O	O	O(N)	O	O	O(S)	
178	Redstart	O	O	m	O	O	O	
	Black Redstart	*(S)	*	*	*(W); O(E)	O	O(S)	
	Robin	*	*	*	*	*	O(S)	
180	Nightingale	O(S)			O	O	O(S)	
	Thrush Nightingale						O	
	Bluethroat	m(E)	m(E)		m	O		
182	Grasshopper Warbler	O	O(S)	O	O	O	O(S)	
	Savi's Warbler	O(S)			O	O(N)		
	Sedge Warbler	O	O	O	O	O	O	
	Aquatic Warbler				O(N)	O(N)		
184	Great Reed Warbler				O	O	O(S)	
	Reed Warbler	O			O	O	O(S)	
	Marsh Warbler	O(S)			O(E)	O	O(S)	
	Cetti's Warbler	*(W)			*	O		
186	Melodious Warbler	m(S)		m(S)	O	O	O(S)	
	Icterine Warbler	m(E)	m(E)	m(S)	m(E)	O		

PP	SPECIES	ENGLAND & WALES	SCOTLAND	IRELAND	FRANCE	GERMANY & BENELUX	SCANDINAVIA	CHECK LIST
186	Barred Warbler	m(E) *(S)	m(E)			O(E)	O(S)	....
	Dartford Warbler				*(W)			....
188	Blackcap	O	O	O	*(W); O(E)	O	O(S)	....
	Orphean Warbler				O(S)	O		....
	Garden Warbler	O	O	O	O	O	O	....
190	Whitethroat	O	O	O	O	O	O(S)	....
	Lesser Whitethroat	O	m		O(E)	O	O(S)	....
	Subalpine Warbler				m(S)			....
192	Willow Warbler	O	O		O	O	O	....
	Chiffchaff	O	O(S)	O	O	O	O(S)	....
	Wood Warbler	O	O	O	O	O	O(S)	....
194	Greenish Warbler						O(E)	....
	Bonelli's Warbler				O(S&W)	O(S)		....
	Arctic Warbler						O(N)	....
196	Yellow-browed Warbler	m(E) *	m *		m *	m *	m(S)	....
	Goldcrest	*(S)	*	*	*		*	....
	Firecrest	*			*	O *		....
	Dunnock	*	*	*	*	*	*(S); O(N)	....

PP	SPECIES	ENGLAND & WALES	SCOTLAND	IRELAND	FRANCE	GERMANY & BENELUX	SCANDINAVIA	CHECK LIST
198	Spotted Flycatcher	O	O	O	O	O	O	
	Pied Flycatcher	O(N&W)	O	m	O(E)	O	O	
	Collared Flycatcher				O(E)	O(S)		
	Red-breasted Flycatcher	m(E)	m		m	O(E)	m(S)	
200	Tawny Pipit	m(E)			O(S&E)	O	O(S)	
	Meadow Pipit	*	*	*	*	*	*(S); O(N)	
	Tree Pipit	O	O	m	O	O	O	
202	Red-throated Pipit					m	O(N)	
	Rock Pipit	*	*	*	*(N&W)	X(N)	*(S); O(N)	
	Water Pipit	X(S)			X	*(S); X(N)		
204	Pied/White Wagtail	*	*	*	*	O	O	
	Grey Wagtail	*	*	*	*	*	O(S)	
	Yellow Wagtail	O	O(S)	m(S)	O	O	O	
206	Great Grey Shrike	X(E)	X		*(E); X(W)	*	*(S); O(N)	
	Lesser Grey Shrike				O(S)	O(S)		
	Woodchat Shrike	O(S)	m(E)		O(S)	O(S)		
	Red-backed Shrike				O	O	O(S)	
208	Waxwing	X(E)	x		x	x	*(N); X(S)	
	Starling	*	*	*	*	*	*(S); O(N)	
	Rose-coloured Starling					m(S)		

257

PP	SPECIES	ENGLAND & WALES	SCOTLAND	IRELAND	FRANCE	GERMANY & BENELUX	SCANDI-NAVIA	CHECK LIST
210	Hawfinch	*			*	*	*(S)	
	Greenfinch	**	**	**	**	**	*(S)	
	Goldfinch	**	**	**	**	**	O(S)	
212	Linnet	*(N); X(E)	***	***	*	*	*(S)	
	Twite	**	**	***	X(N)	X(N)	*(S); O(N)	
	Redpoll	*	*	X	X	X	*(S); O(N)	
	Arctic Redpoll		X				X(N)	
214	Siskin	X	*	*	X	*(S); X(N)	*(S)	
	Citril Finch					*(S)		
	Serin	m(S)			O	O	O(S)	
216	Bullfinch	**	**	**	**	**	*(S)	
	Chaffinch	**	**	**	**	**	*(S); O(N)	
	Brambling	X	X	X	X	X	O(N); X(S)	
218	Scarlet or Common Rosefinch						O(S)	
	Pine Grosbeak						*(N); X(S)	
	Crossbill	*	*	*	*	*	*	
	Parrot Crossbill						*(S)	
	Two-barred Crossbill						m(S)	

PP	SPECIES	ENGLAND & WALES	SCOTLAND	IRELAND	FRANCE	GERMANY & BENELUX	SCANDI- NAVIA	CHECK LIST
220	Corn Bunting	*	*	*	*	*	*(S)	
	Yellowhammer	*	*	*	*	*	*(S); O(N)	
	Cirl Bunting	*(S)	m(E)		*			
	Ortolan Bunting	m(E)			O	O	O(S)	
222	Rock Bunting					*(S)		
	Rustic Bunting						O(N)	
	Little Bunting						O(N)	
	Reed Bunting	*	*	*	*	*	*(S); O(N)	
224	Lapland Bunting	X(E)			X(N)	X(N)	O(N); X(S)	
	Snow Bunting	X	X	X	X(N)	X(N)	*	
	Snow Finch					*(S)		
226	House Sparrow	*	*	*	*	*	*	
	Tree Sparrow	*	*	*	*	*	*(S)	
	Rock Sparrow				*(S)			

259

NOTES

Societies and Journals

The **Royal Society for the Protection of Birds**, The Lodge, Sandy, Bedfordshire, is Britain's largest bird society and is concerned with conservation and education. The society manages numerous reserves throughout the country, the majority of which may be visited on application for a permit. Regional offices in Scotland, Northern Ireland and Wales look after the society's interests in these areas. The society's film unit produces a series of bird films each year which are subsequently available for hire; while the sales department has a wide range of items such as bird books, bird recordings, bird-tables, etc. The RSPB's well-illustrated colour magazine *Birds* is produced quarterly and supplied free to members.

The magazine *Bird Life* is supplied to members of the **Young Ornithologists' Club**, the RSPB's educational club for younger birdwatchers. The club organizes a wide range of local meetings and outings, often combining birdwatching with some additional outdoor activity such as canoeing or rock climbing. A variety of competitions and enquiries suitable for members are organized each year.

The **British Trust for Ornithology**, Beech Grove, Tring, Hertfordshire, is for the more experienced birdwatcher who would like to make his observations available for national use in the many enquiries that the Trust organizes. Examples of these enquiries include the national bird-ringing scheme which provides much information on bird migration; censuses and surveys relating to population and distribution changes; nest record scheme which provides information on breeding success over a large number of years; and numerous detailed enquiries on particular species such as the Heron, Black-headed Gull, etc. Many of the results of these co-ordinated enquiries by amateur birdwatchers are published in the Trust's quarterly journal, *Bird Study*, which is supplied free to members.

The **British Ornithologists' Union**, C/o The Zoological Society of London, Regent's Park, London, NW1 4RY, is Britain's senior ornithological society and is concerned with the scientific study of birds on a world-wide basis. Its quarterly journal, *The Ibis*, contains the results of scientific work and observation and is of primary interest to the expert and professional ornithologist.

The **Council for Nature**, C/o The Zoological Society of London, Regent's Park, London, NW1 4RY, acts as a body to co-ordinate the activities of the many regional societies throughout Britain. Most counties in Britain now have their own bird-watching or natural history society which will be interested in hearing about observations made in their county. Details of these local societies can usually be found in your local library, but if in difficulties, try contacting the Council for Nature.

The **Scottish Ornithologists' Club**, 21 Regent Terrace, Edinburgh, EH7 5BN, and the **Irish Wildbird Conservancy**, C/o Royal Irish Academy, 19 Dawson Street, Dublin 2, are both concerned with the bird life in their respective countries. Both publish journals and reports, *Scottish Birds* and the *Irish Bird Report*.

Two bird journals, unconnected with any society, provide many interesting articles and illustrations for the amateur birdwatcher: *British Birds,* published monthly by Macmillan Journals Ltd, 4 Little Essex Street, London WC2R 3LF, and *World of Birds*, also published monthly by John Grant Publishing Ltd, 6 & 7 Queensthorpe Mews, London, SE26.

Further Reading and Listening

The books and recordings listed below are just a few of the vast numbers of bird publications that are available to assist you in furthering your birdwatching hobby.

Identification Guides
The following three field guides cover a wider geographical area than the present work, and consequently contain several additional species not within the scope of this book. All three are intended simply to help with identification.

Bruun, B., and Singer, A., 1970. *The Hamlyn Guide to Birds of Britain and Europe.* Hamlyn.

Heinzel, H., Fitter, R., and Parslow, J., 1972. *The Birds of Britain and Europe with North Africa and the Middle East.* Collins.

Peterson, R., Mountfort, G., and Hollom, P. A. D., 1974. *A Field Guide to the Birds of Britain and Europe.* 3rd Edition. Collins.

Handbooks
A handbook differs from a field guide in that it contains a considerable amount of additional material to that necessary for identification of a bird. Information usually includes data on breeding, behaviour, migration, display, etc.

Bannerman, D. A., 1953–63. *The Birds of the British Isles.* Vols 1–12. Oliver & Boyd.

Coward, T. A., 1969. *Birds of the British Isles and Their Eggs.* Revised Edition, edited by J. A. G. Barnes. Warne.

Hollom, P. A. D., 1962. *The Popular Handbook of British Birds.* 3rd Edition. Witherby.

Hollom, P. A. D., 1960. *The Popular Handbook of Rarer British Birds.* Witherby.

Witherby, H. F., Jourdain, F. C. R., Ticehurst, N. F., and Tucker, B. W., 1940–41. *The Handbook of British Birds.* Vols 1–5. Witherby.

General and Specific Works
The following titles are a highly selective list from among a wide choice of publications. Many works are rather general in their approach and refer only to the British Isles, but there are a number of books available which deal with foreign birds or the life history of a single species. Amongst the latter are the monograph series in the Collins 'New Naturalist' publications. There are also numerous county avifaunas dealing with the bird life of particular areas of the British Isles.

Campbell, B., and Ferguson-Lees, J., 1972. *A Field Guide to Birds' Nests*. Constable.

Campbell, B., and M. (Editors), 1973. *The Countryman Bird Book*. David & Charles.

Cramp, S., Bourne, W. R. P., and Saunders, D., 1974. *The Seabirds of Britain and Ireland*. Collins.

Darling, L., and L., 1963. *Bird*. Methuen.

Dorst, J., 1962. *The Migrations of Birds*. Heinemann.

Fitter, R. S. R., 1963. *Collins Guide to Bird Watching*. Collins.

Flegg, J., 1973. *Discovering Bird Watching*. Shire.

Gooders, J., 1967. *Where to Watch Birds*. André Deutsch.

Gooders, J., 1974. *Where to Watch Birds in Europe*. André Deutsch.

Parslow, J., 1973. *Breeding Birds of Britain and Ireland*. Poyser.

Soper, T., 1973. *The New Bird Table Book*. David & Charles.

Thomson, A. Landsborough (Editor), 1964. *A New Dictionary of Birds*. Nelson.

Voous, K. H., 1960. *Atlas of European Birds*. Nelson.

Warham, J., 1972. *The Technique of Bird Photography*. Focal Press.

Bird Records

In 1964 Jeffery Boswall published *A Discography of Palaearctic Bird Sound Recordings* as a supplement to the journal *British Birds* in which all the published recordings of the voices of European birds are listed. Amongst the recordings of bird song readily available are:

Bird Sounds in Close Up, Vol. 1
Bird Sounds in Close Up, Vol. 2
A Tapestry of British Bird Song
Witherby's Sound Guide to British Birds
Bird Song Adventure
The Peterson Field Guide to the Bird Songs of Britain and Europe

Index

265

16-25	
26-31	
32-55	
56-71	
72-85	
86-109	
110-129	
130-153	
154-171	
172-181	
182-199	
200-209	
210-227	
228-239	?

DIVERS · GREBES · SHEARWATERS · PETRELS · GANNET · CORMORANTS

HERONS · EGRET · BITTERNS · STORKS · SPOONBILL

DUCKS · GEESE · SWANS

BIRDS OF PREY: EAGLES · BUZZARDS · HAWKS · HARRIERS · OSPREY · FALCONS

GROUSE · PHEASANTS · PARTRIDGES · QUAIL · CRAKES · WATER RAIL · MOORHEN · COOT · CRANE · BUSTARDS

WADERS: OYSTERCATCHER · PLOVERS · SNIPE · CURLEWS · GODWITS · SANDPIPERS · SHANKS · AVOCET · STILT · PHALAROPES

SKUAS · GULLS · TERNS · AUKS

PIGEONS · OWLS · CUCKOO · NIGHTJAR · KINGFISHER · SWIFTS · BEE-EATER · ROLLER · HOOPOE · GOLDEN ORIOLE · WOODPECKERS

LARKS · SWALLOWS · CROWS · TITS · NUTHATCH · CREEPERS · WREN · DIPPER

THRUSHES · CHATS · STARTS · ROBIN · NIGHTINGALES

WARBLERS · CRESTS · DUNNOCK · FLYCATCHERS

PIPITS · WAGTAILS · SHRIKES · WAXWING · STARLINGS

FINCHES · BUNTINGS · SPARROWS

RARITIES